W9-CZV-281

# Microsoft®
# Access 2002

# M I N U T E
# G U I D E

201 West 103rd Street
Indianapolis, IN 46290

**Joe Habraken**

# TEN MINUTE GUIDE TO MICROSOFT® ACCESS 2002

## Copyright © 2002 by Que®

International Standard Book Number: 0-7897-2631-9

Library of Congress Catalog Card Number: 2001090285

Printed in the United States of America

First Printing: August 2001

05  04  03  02    8  7  6

## TRADEMARKS

## WARNING AND DISCLAIMER

**Associate Publisher**
Greg Wiegand

**Acquisitions Editor**
Stephanie J. McComb

**Managing Editor**
Thomas F. Hayes

**Senior Editor**
Susan Ross Moore

**Indexer**
Mandie Frank

**Proofreaders**
Kaylene Riemen
Juli Cook

**Team Coordinator**
Sharry Lee Gregory

**Interior Designer**
Gary Adair

**Cover Designer**
Alan Clements

**Page Layout**
Stacey Richwine-DeRome
Gloria Schurick

# Table of Contents

# ABOUT THE AUTHOR

**Joe Habraken** is a computer technology professional and best-selling author with more than fifteen years of experience in the information technology field as a network administrator, consultant, and educator. His recent publications include *Microsoft Office XP 8-in-1*, *The Absolute Beginner's Guide to Networking (Second Edition)*, and *Practical Cisco Routers*. Joe currently serves as the Director of UNEit, an IT training center for computer industry professionals at the University of New England in Portland, ME.

## DEDICATION

*To all the database users in the world who struggle with information overload.*

## ACKNOWLEDGMENTS

Creating books like this takes a real team effort. I would like to thank Stephanie McComb, our acquisitions editor, who worked very hard to assemble the team that made this book a reality. I would also like to thank our production editor, Susan Moore, who ran the last leg of the race and made sure the book made it to press on time—what a great team of professionals.

# TELL US WHAT YOU THINK!

As the reader of this book, *you* are our most important critic and commentator. We value your opinion and want to know what we're doing right, what we could do better, what areas you'd like to see us publish in, and any other words of wisdom you're willing to pass our way.

As an Associate Publisher for Que, I welcome your comments. You can fax, email, or write me directly to let me know what you did or didn't like about this book—as well as what we can do to make our books stronger.

*Please note that I cannot help you with technical problems related to the topic of this book, and that due to the high volume of mail I receive, I might not be able to reply to every message.*

When you write, please be sure to include this book's title and author as well as your name and phone or fax number. I will carefully review your comments and share them with the author and editors who worked on the book.

Fax:     317-581-4666

E-mail:  feedback@quepublishing.com

Mail:    Associate Publisher
         Que
         201 West 103rd Street
         Indianapolis, IN 46290 USA

# Introduction

Microsoft Access 2002 is a powerful, relational database software package that makes it easy for you to create and manage complex databases. With Access, you can create a database quickly from scratch or by using an Access Database Wizard. Once you've created your database, Access provides all the tools you need to enter and manipulate data.

## THE WHAT AND WHY OF MICROSOFT ACCESS

Access can help you manage any size database, from simple contact lists to complex business databases. Using Microsoft Access, you can do the following:

- Quickly start a new database by using the Database Wizard
- Create tables from scratch or by using a wizard
- Add and edit database information by using both tables and forms
- Manipulate data in a number of tables by using queries and reports

While providing you with many advanced database features, Microsoft Access is built so that even the novice database user can build and maintain a database. This book will help you understand the possibilities awaiting you with Microsoft Access 2002.

## WHY *QUE'S 10 MINUTE GUIDE TO MICROSOFT ACCESS 2002*?

*The 10 Minute Guide to Microsoft Access 2002* can save you precious time while you get to know the different features that Microsoft Access provides. Each lesson is designed to be completed in 10 minutes or less, so you'll be up to snuff on many Access features quickly.

Although you can jump around among lessons, starting at the beginning is a good plan. The bare-bones basics are covered first, and more advanced topics are covered later. If you need help installing Access, see the next section for instructions.

## INSTALLING ACCESS

You can install Microsoft Access 2002 on a computer running Microsoft Windows 98, Windows NT 4.0, Windows 2000, and Windows XP. Microsoft Access can be installed as a stand-alone product and is also available as part of the Microsoft Office XP suite (both of these flavors of Access come on a CD-ROM).

To install Access, follow these steps:

1. Start your computer. Then insert the Microsoft Access or Microsoft XP Office CD in the CD-ROM drive. The CD-ROM should autostart, providing you with the opening installation screen.

2. If the CD-ROM does not autostart, choose Start, Run. In the Run dialog box, type the letter of the CD-ROM drive, followed by **setup** (for example, **e:\setup**). If necessary, use the Browse button to locate and select the CD-ROM drive and the setup.exe program.

3. When the Setup Wizard prompts you, enter your name, organization, and CD key in the appropriate box.

4. Choose **Next** to continue.

5. The next Wizard screen provides instructions to complete the installation. After providing the appropriate information on each screen, select **Next** to advance from screen to screen.

After you complete the installation from the CD, icons for Access and any other Office applications you might have installed will be provided

on the Windows Start menu. Lesson 2 in this book provides you with a
step-by-step guide to starting Access 2002.

## CONVENTIONS USED IN THIS BOOK

To help you move through the lessons easily, these conventions are
used:

| | |
|---|---|
| **On-screen text** | On-screen text appears in bold type. |
| **Text you should type** | Information you need to type appears in a different bold, typeface. |
| **Items you select** | Commands, options, and icons you are to select and keys you are to press appear in bold type. |

In telling you to choose menu commands, this book uses the format
*menu title, menu command.* For example, the statement "choose File,
Properties" means to "open the File menu and select the Properties
command."

In addition to those conventions, the *10 Minute Guide to Microsoft
Access 2002* uses the following icons to identify helpful information:

**PLAIN ENGLISH**

> **terms**   New or unfamiliar terms are defined in term
> sidebars.

**TIP**

> **Tips**   Read these tips for ideas that cut corners and
> confusion.

**CAUTION**

> **Cautions**   This icon identifies areas where new users
> often run into trouble; these cautions offer practical
> solutions to those problems.

# Lesson 1
# What's New in Access 2002

*In this lesson, you are introduced to Microsoft Access and you learn what's new in Access 2002.*

## Understanding Access 2002

Strictly speaking, a *database* is any collection of information. Your local telephone book, for example, is a database, as is the shopping list that you take to the grocery store. Microsoft Access makes creating databases very straightforward and relatively simple.

The electronic container that Access provides for holding your data is called a *table* (see Figure 1.1). A table consists of rows and columns. Access stores each database entry (for example, each employee or each inventory item) in its own row; this is a *record*. Each record contains specific information related to one person, place, or thing.

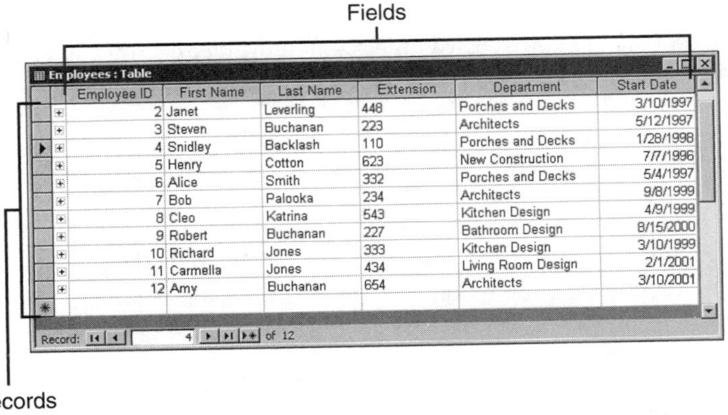


| Employee ID | First Name | Last Name | Extension | Department | Start Date |
|---|---|---|---|---|---|
| 2 | Janet | Leverling | 448 | Porches and Decks | 3/10/1997 |
| 3 | Steven | Buchanan | 223 | Architects | 5/12/1997 |
| 4 | Snidley | Backlash | 110 | Porches and Decks | 1/28/1998 |
| 5 | Henry | Cotton | 623 | New Construction | 7/7/1996 |
| 6 | Alice | Smith | 332 | Porches and Decks | 5/4/1997 |
| 7 | Bob | Palooka | 234 | Architects | 9/8/1999 |
| 8 | Cleo | Katrina | 543 | Kitchen Design | 4/9/1999 |
| 9 | Robert | Buchanan | 227 | Bathroom Design | 8/15/2000 |
| 10 | Richard | Jones | 333 | Kitchen Design | 3/10/1999 |
| 11 | Carmella | Jones | 434 | Living Room Design | 2/1/2001 |
| 12 | Amy | Buchanan | 654 | Architects | 3/10/2001 |

**FIGURE 1.1**
*A table serves as the container for your database information.*

**PLAIN ENGLISH**

**Table**    A container for your database information consisting of columns and rows.

Each record is broken up into discrete pieces of information, called fields. Each *field* consists of a separate column in the table. Each field contains a different piece of information that taken all together makes up a particular record. For example, Last Name is a field. All the last names in the entire table (all in the same column) are collectively known as the Last Name field.

**PLAIN ENGLISH**

**Record**    A row in a table that contains information about a particular person, place, or thing.

**PLAIN ENGLISH**

**Field**    A discrete piece of information making up a record. Each column in the Access table is a different field.

## INTRODUCING OTHER ACCESS OBJECTS

The table is just one type of object found in Access. You can also work with forms, queries, and reports.

- A *form* is used to enter, edit, and view data in a table, one record at a time.

- A *query* enables you to ask your database questions. The answer to the query can be used to manipulate data in a table, such as deleting records or viewing the data in a table that meets only certain criteria.

- A *report* enables you to summarize database information in a format that is suitable for printing.

In essence, each of these different database objects allows you a different way of viewing and manipulating the data found in your tables. Each of these objects (including the table) should also be considered as you plan a new database. Planning a new database is discussed in Lesson 2, "Working in Access."

## WHAT'S NEW IN ACCESS 2002

Access 2002 is similar in look and feel to Access 2000 the previous version of this powerful database software. Access 2002 provides the same adaptive menu and toolbar system found in Access 2000 that customizes the commands and icons listed on your menus and toolbars based on the commands you use most frequently.

Access 2002 also provides you with other useful tools and features that were available in previous versions of the Access software. For example, tools such as the Database and Tables Wizards make it easy for you to quickly create your databases and the tables that will contain your data.

**PLAIN ENGLISH**

**Wizard**   A feature that guides you step by step through a particular process in Access, such as creating a new table.

While providing you with the familiar tools and features found in earlier versions of Access, Access 2002 also supplies several new features. For example, Access 2002 now provides you with the ability to undo and redo multiple actions when you work with Access database objects such as tables and forms in the design view.

Other new features in Access 2002 such as Task panes and Voice dictation make it even easier for you to create and maintain your database files. Let's take a look at some of the important changes to the Access 2002 software.

## INTRODUCING TASK PANES

One of the biggest changes to the Access environment (and all the Microsoft Office XP suite applications such as Word 2002, Excel 2002 and PowerPoint 2002) is the introduction of the Office task pane. The task pane is a special pane that appears on the right side of the Access application window when you use certain Access features (features that were formerly controlled using dialog boxes).

For example, when you choose to start a new database, the New File task pane appears (see Figure 1.2). This task pane makes it easy for you to start a new blank database or create a database using the different database templates provided by Access. Creating a new database in Access is covered in Lesson 3, "Creating a New Database."

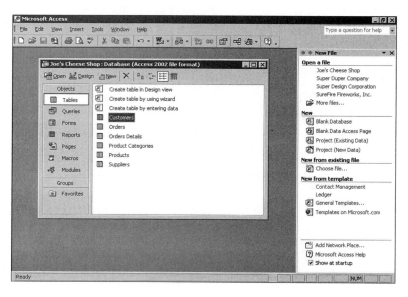

**FIGURE 1.2**
*The New File task pane makes it easy for you to create a new Access database.*

Other task panes that you will run across as you work in Access are the Office Clipboard and the Clip Gallery. The Office Clipboard allows you to copy or cut multiple items from an Access object such as a table and then paste them into new locations. The Clip Gallery provides you with the ability to insert clip art and other images into your Access tables, forms, or reports. Task panes are discussed in this book when appropriate as you explore the various Access features.

## INTRODUCING VOICE DICTATION AND VOICE COMMANDS

One of the most exciting new features in Access 2002 (and the entire Office XP suite) is voice dictation and voice-activated commands. If your computer is outfitted with a sound card, speakers, and a microphone (or a microphone with an earphone headset), you can dictate information into your Access tables. You also can use voice commands to activate the menu system and toolbars in Access.

Before you can really take advantage of the Speech feature, you must provide it with some training so that it can more easily recognize your speech patterns and intonation. After the Speech feature is trained, you can effectively use it to dictate text entries or access various application commands without a keyboard or mouse.

> **CAUTION**
>
> **Requirements for Getting the Most Out of the Speech Feature**    To make the Speech feature useful, you will need a fairly high-quality microphone. Microsoft suggests a microphone/headset combination. The Speech feature also requires a more powerful computer. Microsoft suggests using a computer with 128MB of RAM and a Pentium II (or later) processor running at a minimum of 400MHz. A computer that meets or exceeds these higher standards should be capable of getting the most out of the Speech feature.

You may wish to explore the other lessons in this book if you are new to Access before you attempt to use the Speech feature. Having a good understanding of how Access operates and the features that it provides will allow you to then get the most out of using the Speech feature.

## TRAINING THE SPEECH FEATURE

The first time you start the Speech feature in Access, you are required to configure and train the feature. Follow these steps to get the Speech feature up and running:

1. In Access, select the **Tools** menu and select **Speech**. The Welcome to Office Speech Recognition dialog box appears. To begin the process of setting up your microphone and training the Speech feature, click the **Next** button.

2. The first screen of the Microphone Wizard appears. It asks you to make sure that your microphone and speakers are connected to your computer. If you have a headset microphone, this screen shows you how to adjust the microphone for use. Click **Next** to continue.

3. The next wizard screen asks you to read a short text passage so that your microphone volume level can be adjusted (see Figure 1.3). When you have finished reading the text, click **Next** to continue.

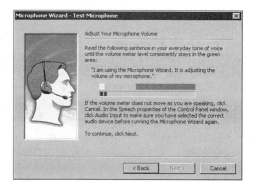

**FIGURE 1.3**
*The Microphone Wizard adjusts the volume of your microphone.*

4. On the next screen, you are told that if you have a headset microphone, you can click **Finish** and proceed to the speech recognition training. If you have a different type of microphone, you are asked to read another text passage. The text is then played back to you. This is to determine whether the microphone is placed at an appropriate distance from your mouth; when you get a satisfactory playback, click **Finish**.

When you finish working with the Microphone Wizard, the Voice Training Wizard appears. This wizard collects samples of your speech and, in essence, educates the Speech feature as to how you speak.

To complete the voice training process, follow these steps:

1. After reading the information on the opening screen, click **Next** to begin the voice training process.

2. On the next screen, you are asked to provide your gender and age (see Figure 1.4). After specifying the correct information, click **Next**.

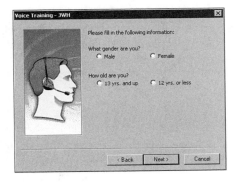

**FIGURE 1.4**
*Supply the voice trainer with your gender and age.*

3. On the next wizard screen, you are provided an overview of how the voice training will proceed. You are also provided with directions for how to pause the training session. Click **Next**.

4.  The next wizard screen reminds you to adjust your microphone. You are also reminded that you need a quiet room when training the Speech feature. When you are ready to begin training the speech recognition feature, click **Next**.

5.  On the next screen, you are asked to read some text. As the wizard recognizes each word, the word is highlighted. After finishing with this screen, continue by clicking **Next**.

6.  You are asked to read text on several subsequent screens. Words are selected as the wizard recognizes them.

7.  When you complete the training screens, your profile is updated. Click **Finish** on the wizard's final screen.

You are now ready to use the Speech feature. The next two sections discuss using the Voice Dictation and Voice Command features.

**CAUTION**

**The Speech Feature Works Better Over Time**    Be advised that the voice feature's performance improves as you use it. As you learn to pronounce your words more carefully, the Speech feature tunes itself to your speech patterns. You might need to do additional training sessions to fine-tune the Speech feature.

## USING VOICE DICTATION

When you are ready to start dictating text into an Access table, put on your headset microphone or place your standalone microphone in the proper position that you determined when you used the Microphone Wizard. When you're ready to go, select the **Tools** menu and then select **Speech**. The Language bar appears, as shown in Figure 1.5. If necessary, click the **Dictation** button on the toolbar (if the Dictation button is not already activated or depressed).

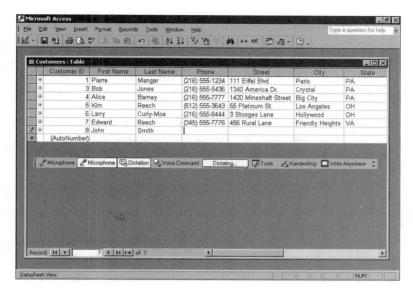

**FIGURE 1.5**
*Dictating text into an Access table.*

After you enable the Dictation button, you can begin dictating your text. Figure 1.5 shows text being dictated into an Access table. When you want to move to the next field in the record that you are dictating, say "tab." Numbers are dictated as they appear; for example, if you wished to enter the phone number prefix of 555, you would say "555." If you need to put a line break into the text, say "new line." Punctuation is placed into a table (in cases where you are creating a field that requires punctuation marks) by saying the name of a particular punctuation mark, such as "period" or "comma."

**CAUTION**

**How Do I Insert the Word "Comma" Rather Than the Punctuation Mark?**    Because certain keywords, such as "period" or "comma," are used to insert punctuation during dictation, you must spell these words out if you want to include them in the text. To do this, say "spelling mode," and then spell out the word, such as c-o-m-m-a. As soon as you dictate an entire word, the spelling mode is ended.

When you have finished dictating into the document, click the **Microphone** button on the Language bar (the second Microphone button from the left; the first is used to select the current speech driver, which you can leave as the default). When you click the **Microphone** button, the Language bar collapses, hiding the **Dictation** and the **Voice Command** buttons. You can also stop Dictation mode by saying "microphone."

You can minimize the Language bar by clicking the **Minimize** button on the right end of the bar. This sends the Language bar to the Windows System Tray (it appears as a small square icon marked EN, if you are using the English version of Office and Access).

With the Language bar minimized in the System Tray, you can quickly open it when you need it. Click the **Language Bar** icon in the System Tray, and then select **Show the Language Bar**.

Using the Dictation feature correctly requires that you know how to get the Speech feature to place the correct text or characters into your Access table. For more help with the dictation feature, consult the Microsoft Access Help system (discussed in Lesson 10).

## USING VOICE COMMANDS

Another tool the Speech feature provides is voice commands. You can open and select menus in Access and even navigate dialog boxes using voice commands.

To use voice commands, open the Language bar (click **Tools,** **Speech**). Click the **Microphone** icon, if necessary, to expand the Language bar. Then, click the **Voice Command** icon on the bar (or say "voice command").

To open a particular menu such as the Format menu, say "format." Then, to open a particular submenu such as Font, say "font." In the case of these voice commands, the Font dialog box opens.

You can then navigate a particular dialog box using voice commands. In the Font dialog box, for example, to change the size of the font, say "size"; this activates the Size box that controls font size. Then, say the size of the font, such as "14." You can also activate other font attributes in the dialog box in this manner. Say the name of the area of the dialog box you want to use, and then say the name of the feature you want to turn on or select.

When you have finished working with a particular dialog box, say "OK," (or "Cancel" or "Apply," as needed) and the dialog box closes and provides you with the features you selected in the dialog box. When you have finished using voice commands, say "microphone," or click the **Microphone** icon on the Language bar.

Believe it or not, you can also activate buttons on the various toolbars using voice commands. For example, you could sort your Access table by a particular field by clicking in that field and then saying "sort ascending." The Sort Ascending button on the Table Datasheet toolbar becomes active and your table is sorted by the selected field.

In this lesson, you were introduced to Access 2002 and some of the new features available in this latest version of Microsoft Access such as task panes and the Speech feature. In the next lesson, you learn how to plan an Access database and start the Access software.

# LESSON 2
# Working in Access

*In this lesson, you learn what a relational database is and how to plan your database. You also learn how to start Microsoft Access, become familiar with its toolbars, and then exit the software.*

## PLANNING A DATABASE

Access is a special kind of database called a *relational database*. A relational database divides information into discrete subsets. Each subset groups information by a particular theme, such as customer information, sales orders, or product information. In Access, these subsets of data reside in individual tables like the one described previously.

Access enables you to build relationships between tables. These relationships are based on a field that is common to two tables. Each table must have a field called the primary key (you learn how to specify a field as the primary key in Lessons 4 and 5). The primary key must uniquely identify each record in the table. So, the primary key field is typically a field that assigns a unique number (no duplicates within that table) to each record.

For example, a Customers table might contain a Customer Identification field (shown as CustomerID in Figure 2.1) that identifies each customer by a unique number (such as your Social Security number). You might also have a table that holds all your sales orders. To link the Sales table to the Customers table, you include the Customer Identification field in the Sales table. This identifies each sale by customer and links the Sales table data to the Customers table data.

## PLAIN ENGLISH

> **Relational Database**  A collection of individual tables holding discrete subsets of information that are linked by common data fields.

You will find that even a simple database consists of several tables that are related. Figure 2.1 shows a database and the different table relationships. Lesson 11, "Creating Relationships Between Tables," provides information on creating table relationships.

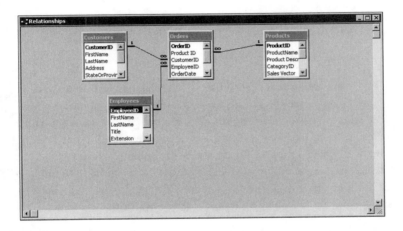

**FIGURE 2.1**
*A relational database contains related tables.*

When you do create a new database, you want to make sure that the database is designed not only to meet your data entry needs, but also to meet your needs for viewing and reporting the data that is held in the various tables that make up the database. Taking a little time to plan your database before you create it can save you from headaches down the road. The sections that follow provide some tips on planning a database.

## DETERMINING YOUR TABLES

Technically, you need only one table to make a database. However, because Access is a relational database program, it's meant to handle many tables and create relationships among them. For example, in a database that keeps track of customer orders, you might have the following tables:

- Customers

- Orders

- Products

- Salespeople

- Shipping Methods

Using many tables that hold subsets of the database information can help you avoid making redundant data entries. For example, suppose you want to keep contact information on your customers along with a record of each transaction they make. If you kept it all in one table, you would have to repeat the customer's full name, address, and phone number each time you entered a new transaction. It would also be a nightmare if the customer's address changed; you would have to change the address in every transaction record for that customer.

A better way is to assign each customer an ID number. Include that ID number in a table that contains names and addresses, and then use the same ID number as a link to a separate transactions table. Basically, then, each table in your database should have a particular theme—for example, Employee Contact Information or Customer Transactions. Don't try to have more than one theme per table.

A table design requirement is to be sure that every table that you create uses the first field (the first column of the table) as a way to uniquely identify each record in the table. This field can then serve as the table's primary key. For example, customers can be assigned a customer number, or sales transactions can be assigned a transaction number. The primary key is the only way that you can then link the table to another table in the database.

It's a good idea to do some work on paper and jot down a list of tables that will be contained in the database and the fields that they will contain. Restructuring tables because of poor planning isn't impossible, but it isn't much fun, either.

## DETERMINING YOUR FORMS

As already mentioned in Lesson 1, forms are used for data entry. They allow you to enter data one record at a time (see Figure 2.2). Complex forms can also be constructed that actually allow you to enter data into more than one table at a time (this is because fields can be pulled from several tables in the same database into one form).

**FIGURE 2.2**
*A form allows you to enter data one record at a time.*

Planning the forms that you use for data entry is not as crucial as planning the tables that make up the database. Forms should be designed to make data entry easier. They are great in that they allow you to concentrate on the entry or editing of data one record at a time. You might want to have a form for each table in the database, or you might want to create composite forms that allow you to enter data into the form that is actually deposited into more than one table.

The great thing about forms is that they don't have to contain all the fields that are in a particular table. For example, if you have someone else enter the data that you keep in an employee database, but you don't want that data entry person to see the employee salaries, you can design a form that does not contain the salary field.

## DETERMINING YOUR QUERIES

Queries enable you to manipulate the data in your database tables. A query can contain criteria that allow you to delete old customer records, or it can provide you with a list of employees who have worked at the company for more than 10 years.

Deciding the queries that you will use before all the data is entered can be difficult. However, if you are running a store—a cheese shop, for example—and know that it is important for you to keep close tabs on your cheese inventory, you will probably want to build some queries to track sales and inventory.

Queries are an excellent way for you to determine the status of your particular endeavor. For example, you could create a query to give you total sales for a particular month. Queries are, in effect, questions. Use queries to get the answers that you need from your database information.

## DETERMINING YOUR REPORTS

A report is used to publish the data in the database. It places the data on the page (or pages) in a highly readable format. Reports are meant to be printed (unlike tables and forms, which are usually used onscreen). For example, you might run a club and want a report of all people who haven't paid their membership dues or who owe more than $1,000 on their account.

A report is usually for the benefit of other people who aren't sitting with you at your computer. For example, you might print a report to hand out to your board of directors to encourage them to keep you on as CEO. A report can pull data from many tables at once, perform calculations on the data (such as summing or averaging), and present you with neatly formatted results. Figure 2.3 shows a database report.

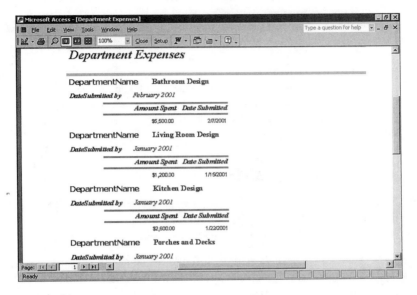

**FIGURE 2.3**
*Reports allow you to organize and summarize database information.*

You can create new reports at any time; you don't have to plan them before you create your database. However, if you know you will want a certain report, you might design your tables in the format that will be most effective for that report's use.

Designing good databases is an acquired skill. The more databases that you work with, the better each will be. Now that you've gotten your feet wet with database planning, take a look at how to start Access.

## STARTING ACCESS

You can start Access in several ways, depending on how you've instal-led it. One way is to use the Start menu button. Follow these steps:

1. Click the **Start** button. A menu appears.

2. Highlight or point to **Programs**. A list of programs installed on your computer appears.

3. Click **Microsoft Access** in the list of applications. Access starts.

**PLAIN ENGLISH**

> **Moving Programs Around on the Start Menu**    If you prefer to have Access in a different program group, open the **Start** menu and drag the Access item to another location of your choice.

## OTHER WAYS TO START ACCESS

Some other ways to start Access require more knowledge of Windows and Microsoft Office. If you're confused by them, stick with the primary method explained in the preceding section.

- You can create a shortcut icon for Access that sits on your desktop; you can then start Access by double-clicking the icon. To create the shortcut icon, drag the Access item from the **Start** menu to the desktop.

- When you're browsing files in Windows Explorer, you can double-click any Access data file to start Access and open that data file. Access data files have an .mdb extension and a little icon next to them that resembles the icon next to Microsoft Access on the Programs menu.

- If you can't find Access, you can search for it. Click the Start button and select **Find**, select **Files or Folders**, and then type msaccess.exe into the Named text box. Open the **Look In** list and select **My Computer**. Then click **Find Now**. When the file appears on the list at the bottom of the Find window, double-click it to start Access, or right-click and drag it to the desktop to create an Access shortcut.

# PARTS OF THE ACCESS SCREEN

Access is much like any other Windows program: It contains menus, toolbars, a status bar, the Ask a Question box, and so on. Figure 2.4 provides a look at these different areas of the Access window. This view assumes that you have either created a new database or opened an existing database in the Access workspace. Creating a new database and opening an existing database are discussed in Lesson 3, "Creating a New Database."

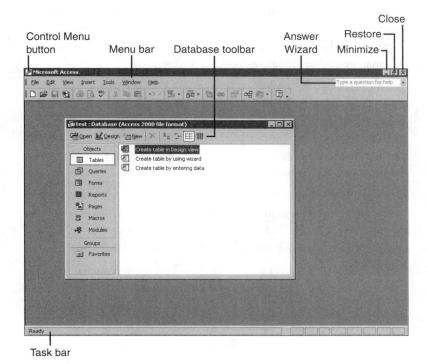

**FIGURE 2.4**
*Access provides the familiar menu and toolbars found in all Microsoft Office applications.*

You probably have noticed that most of the buttons on the toolbar are unavailable. That's because you haven't created any objects, such as tables or forms, for the new database. The toolbar currently displayed in the Access window is the Database toolbar. Access actually has a different toolbar for each database object such as a table or a form. In some cases, multiple toolbars exist for an object, depending on whether you are entering data into the object or changing the design parameters of the object.

For example, Access tables have two toolbars. The Table Datasheet toolbar provides you with tools that help you enter and manipulate the data in the table when you work with it in the Datasheet view. If you switch to the Design view of the table, a Table Design toolbar helps you manipulate the design settings for the table.

Because you will be working with each Access object type, you will also become familiar with each object toolbar. As you work with the various buttons on the toolbars, remember that you can place the mouse pointer on any toolbar button to receive a ToolTip. The ToolTip provides the name of the button, which usually is indicative of what the particular tool is used for.

One other thing that should be mentioned related to the Access window is that only one database at a time can be open in the Access window. It doesn't enable you to work on multiple databases at the same time, as you could work with multiple documents, or workbooks in Word or Excel.

### PLAIN ENGLISH

**Choose Your Toolbars**    As you work in Access on the various objects, right-click any toolbar to view a shortcut menu that provides a list of available toolbars. Typically, you are limited to the toolbar specific to the object that you are working on.

# EXITING ACCESS

Although you have only barely gotten your feet wet with Access, take a look at how you exit the application. You can exit Access in several ways:

- Select **File**, and then select **Exit**.

- Click the Access window's **Close** (x) button on the upper right of the Access window.

- Press **Alt+F4**.

In this lesson, you became familiar with what a relational database is and how to plan the various types of objects that would be placed in a new database. You also had a chance to open Access, take a look at the Access window and exit the application window. In the next lesson, we look at different ways to create a new Access database.

# LESSON 3
# Creating a New Database

*In this lesson, you learn how to create a blank database. You also learn how to create a new database using a database template and the Database Wizard. You also learn how to close your database, open it, and how to find a misplaced database file.*

## CHOOSING HOW TO CREATE YOUR DATABASE

Before you can create your database tables and actually enter data, you must create a database file. The database is really just a container file that holds all the database objects, such as the tables, forms, and reports. You also have two options for creating a new database: You can create a blank database from scratch or create a new database based on a database template.

Creating a new database based on a template means that you take advantage of the Database Wizard, which not only creates your new database file but also helps you quickly create tables, forms, and other objects for the database.

### PLAIN ENGLISH

**Database Wizard** Access provides several templates for creating new database files, and the Database Wizard walks you through the process of creating objects, such as tables, for the new database.

Whether you create your new database from scratch or use one of the database templates depends on how closely one of the Access templates meets your database needs. If one of the templates provides you with the type of tables and other objects necessary for your project, it makes sense to use a template. For example, if you want to create a database that helps you manage your company's inventory, you can take advantage of the Inventory Control template that Access provides. This template provides you with the basic tables and other objects to start the process of getting a handle on your inventory database.

In some cases, the templates might not meet your needs. For example, if you want to create a complex database that allows you to track sales, customers, and employee performance, it might be easier to create a blank database and then create each table for the database from scratch. Let's start the overview of database creation with creating a blank database.

## SELECTING A DATABASE FILE TYPE

One thing to discuss before you look at creating a new database is the database file format. By default, new databases created in Access 2002 are created in the Access 2000 file format. This makes your database files compatible with earlier versions of Access, such as Access 2000 and Access 97.

Saving the database in the Access 2000 file format does not negate you from using any of the tools or features available in Access 2002. If you use your database files only in Access 2002 and share the databases with co-workers who also use Access 2002, you can set the default file format for new databases to Access 2002. Select the **Tools** menu, and then select **Options**. The Options dialog box opens.

Select the **Advanced** tab on the Options dialog box. Click the **Default File Format** drop-down box and select **Access 2002**. Now take a look at creating new databases.

## CREATING A BLANK DATABASE

Creating a blank database is very straightforward. As mentioned previously, you are just creating the container file that holds all the objects that actually make up the database. To create a blank database, follow these steps:

1. Open the Access window (click **Start**, **Programs**, **Access**).

2. Select **Blank Database** in the task pane or click the **New** button on the Database toolbar. The File New Database dialog box appears (see Figure 3.1).

**FIGURE 3.1**
*Provide a location and a name for the new database file.*

3. Use the Save In drop-down box to locate the folder in which you want to save the new database. Type a name for the new file into the **File Name** text box.

4. When you are ready to create the database file, click **Create**. The new database window appears in the Access workspace (see Figure 3.2).

Object icons                     Object pane

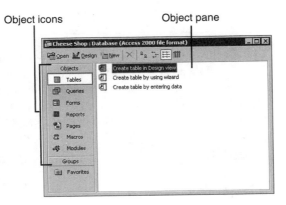

**FIGURE 3.2**
*A new database window opens in Access.*

The database window provides you with a set of icons that allows you to select a particular object type. For example, the Tables icon is selected by default after you create the new database (which makes sense, because you need to create at least one table before you can create any of the other object types such as a form or a report).

Shortcuts for different methods of creating tables are provided at the top of the Object pane on the right side of the database window. After you create a new table for the database, it is listed in this pane. In Lesson 4, "Creating a Table with the Table Wizard," and Lesson 5, "Creating a Table from Scratch," you take a look at creating tables.

The database window enables you to view the different objects that you've created for a particular database (or those that have been created when you use the Database Wizard). When you want to switch the database window's focus to a different Access object, all you have to do is click the appropriate icon in the Objects list.

**TIP**

> **Different Ways to View the Database Windows**    The tool-
> bar on the database window provides buttons for open-
> ing or creating a particular database object, such as a
> table or a form. The toolbar also provides buttons that
> can be used to change the view in the Object pane:
> **Large Icons**, **Small Icons**, **List** (the default view) and
> **Details** (which provides information such as when the
> object was last modified).

## CLOSING A DATABASE

When you finish working with a database, you might want to close it
so that you can concentrate on creating a new database (such as you
do in the next section). However, because Access allows you to have
only one database open at a time, as soon as you begin creating a new
database the currently open database closes. Opening an existing database also closes the current database (which is something you do later
in this lesson).

If you want to close a database, there are a couple of possibilities: You
can click the **Close** (x) button on the database window, or you can
select **File**, **Close**. In either case, the database window closes, clearing
the Access workspace.

## CREATING A DATABASE FROM A TEMPLATE

Another option for creating a new database is using one of the Access
database templates. Templates are available for asset tracking, contact
management, inventory control, and other database types. Another
perk of using an Access template to create a new database is that a
Database Wizard creates tables and other objects, such as forms and
reports, for the new database. The wizard also sets up the relationships
between the various tables (making your database relational).

Your interaction with the Database Wizard is somewhat limited; the
wizard allows you to select the fields that will be used in the tables

that it creates for the database. However, you don't have a say about which tables are initially created (tables can always be deleted later if you don't need them). You are, however, given the opportunity to select the format for screen displays (for forms and reports) and to select the format for printed reports.

To create a database from a template, follow these steps:

1. In the Access window, click **General Templates** on the task pane. If the task pane is not currently in the Access window, select **File**, **New** to open it.

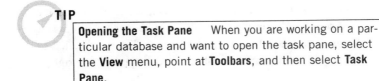

**TIP**

**Opening the Task Pane**    When you are working on a particular database and want to open the task pane, select the **View** menu, point at **Toolbars**, and then select **Task Pane**.

2. The Templates dialog box appears. If necessary, click the Databases tab on the dialog box to view the database templates (see Figure 3.3).

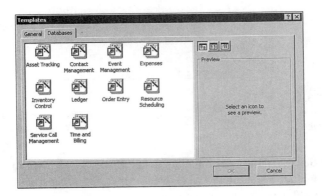

**FIGURE 3.3**
*Access provides several database templates.*

**3.** Click the database template you want to use (for example, the Contact Management template) and then click **OK**. The File New Database dialog box appears.

**4.** Specify a location for the database using the Save In drop-down list, type a name for the database, and then click **Create** to continue. A new database file is created, and then the Database Wizard associated with the template starts. For example, if you chose the Contact Management template, the wizard appears and explains the type of information that the database holds.

**5.** To move past the wizard's opening screen, click **Next**. On the next screen, a list of the tables that will be created appears (see Figure 3.4). The tables in the database are listed on the left of the screen and the selected table's fields appear on the right.

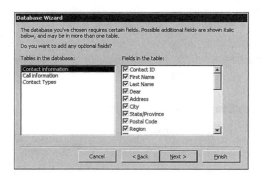

**FIGURE 3.4**
*You can examine and deselect (or select) the fields that will be contained in each table.*

**6.** Select a table to examine its fields. If you do not want to include a field in the table, clear the check box next to the field name. Optional fields are also listed for each field and are shown in italic. To include an optional field, click it to place a check mark next to it. When you have finished viewing the tables and their fields, click **Next** to continue.

**CAUTION**

**Be Careful Deselecting Fields!**    Because you are stuck with the tables that the Database Wizard creates, you must be very careful removing fields from the tables. This is especially true of fields that uniquely identify the records in a table, such as Contact ID. These fields are often used to relate the tables in the database. You might want to leave all the fields alone initially when you use the wizard.

7. The next screen asks you to select the screen display style you want to use. This affects how forms appear on the screen. Click a display style in the list to preview the style; after selecting the style you want to use, click **Next**.

8. On the next screen, the wizard asks you for a style for your printed reports. Click a report style and examine the preview of it. When you decide on a style, click it, and then click **Next**.

**TIP**

**Report Background**    The colored backgrounds used for some report styles look nice onscreen, but they don't print well on a black-and-white printer. Unless you have access to a color printer, stick to plain backgrounds for the best report printouts.

9. On the next wizard screen, you are asked to provide a title for the database. This title appears on reports and can be different from the filename. Enter a title as shown in Figure 3.5.

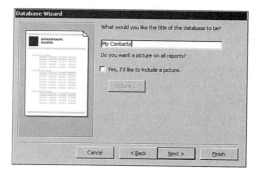

**FIGURE 3.5**
*Enter a title for the database, and as an option, choose a graphic to use for a logo.*

**10.** (Optional) To include a picture on your forms and reports (for example, your company's logo), click the **Yes, I'd Like to Include a Picture** check box. Then click the **Picture** button, choose a picture file from your hard drive (or other source), and click **OK** to return to the wizard.

**11.** Click **Next** to continue. You are taken to the last wizard screen; click **Finish** to open the new database. The wizard goes to work creating your database and its database objects.

When the wizard has finished creating the database, the database's Main Switchboard window appears (see Figure 3.6). The Main Switchboard opens automatically whenever you open the database.

All the databases created using one of the Access templates (other than the Blank Database template) include a Main Switchboard. The Switchboard is nothing more than a fancy form with some programming built in to it. It enables you to perform common tasks related to database management by clicking a button. It is very useful when a person is unfamiliar with how to manipulate the various objects in a database.

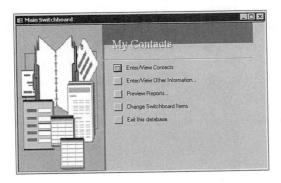

**FIGURE 3.6**
*The Switchboard window is a database navigation tool provided by the Database Wizard.*

Using the Main Switchboard is pretty much self-explanatory. After you become familiar with Access, you probably won't even use it. To close the Switchboard, click its **Close (x)** button.

**TIP**

**I Hate That Switchboard!**    To prevent the Switchboard from opening when you open the database, choose **Tools, Startup**. In the Startup dialog box, select the **Display Form/Page** drop-down list and select **[None]**. Click **OK**.

After you close the Switchboard window, you will find that the database window has been minimized in the Access workspace. Just double-click its title bar (at the bottom-left corner of the screen) to open it. To see the tables that the wizard created, click the **Tables** object type. Click the other object types (such as forms) to see the other objects that were created by the wizard.

The tables that the wizard creates are, of course, empty. After you fill them with data (either inputting the data directly into the table or using a form), you will be able to run queries and create reports.

## OPENING A DATABASE

You have already taken a look at how to close a database; next, you walk through the process of opening a database file. The next time you start Access or after you finish working with another database, you need to know how to open your other database files.

One of the easiest ways to open a database you've recently used is to select it from the File menu. Follow these steps:

1.  Open the **File** menu. You'll see up to four databases that you've recently used listed at the bottom of the menu.

2.  If the database you need is listed there, click it.

**TIP**

> **Want to See More Files?**   To increase the number of files displayed in this list, open the **Tools** menu and select **Options**. Then, from the **General** tab of the Options dialog box, select a number from 1 to 9 (the default is 4) in the **Recently Used Files** drop-down list.

A list of recently used databases also appears on the tip of the Access task pane. You can open any of the files by clicking the filename (to open the task pane, select **View, Toolbars, Task Pane**).

If a file you want to open is not listed either on the File menu or the task pane, you can open it using the Open command. Follow these steps:

1.  Select **File, Open,** or click the toolbar's **Open** button. The Open dialog box appears (see Figure 3.7).

**FIGURE 3.7**
*Use the Open dialog box to locate a database file you want to open.*

2. If the file isn't in the currently displayed folder, use the Look In drop-down list to access the correct drive, and then double-click folders displayed in the dialog box to locate the file.

3. When you have located the database file, double-click the file to open it.

In this lesson, you learned how to create a database from scratch and how to create a database from a template. You also learned how to close and open a database. In the next lesson, you learn how to create a table using the Table Wizard.

# LESSON 4

# Creating a Table with the Table Wizard

*In this lesson, you learn how to create a table by using the Table Wizard.*

## TABLES ARE ESSENTIAL

As discussed in Lesson 1, your tables really provide the essential framework for your database. Tables not only hold the data that you enter into the database, but they are designed so that relationships can be established between the various tables in the database. Tables can be created from scratch, as discussed in the next lesson, or they can be created using the Table Wizard.

## WORKING WITH THE TABLE WIZARD

The Table Wizard can save you a lot of time by supplying you with all the needed fields and field formats for entering your database information. Access provides a large number of different kinds of tables that you can create with the wizard. The wizard is also fairly flexible, allowing you to select the fields the table will contain and the way in which they will be arranged. You can also change the name of a field during the process. If the wizard doesn't provide a particular field, you can always add it to the table later, as discussed in Lesson 6, "Editing a Table's Structure."

To create a table using the Table Wizard, follow these steps:

1. In the database window, click the **Tables** object icon, and then double-click **Create Table by Using Wizard**. The Table Wizard opens.

TIP

> **Alternative Routes**    You can also start the Table Wizard by clicking the **New** button in the database window or choosing **Insert, Table**. In both cases, the New Table dialog box opens. Then, choose **Table Wizard** and click **OK**.

2. On the first Table Wizard screen, you can select from two categories of table types: **Business** or **Personal**. Your choice determines the list of sample tables that appears (see Figure 4.1).

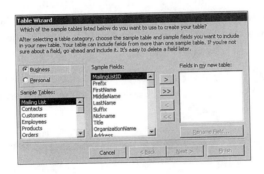

**FIGURE 4.1**
*Select either the Business or Personal category to view a list of tables.*

3. Select a table in the Sample Tables list; its fields appear in the Sample Fields list.

4. To include a field from the Sample Fields list in the table, select the field and click the **Add (>)** button to move it to the **Fields in My New Table** list. You can include all the fields in Sample Fields list by clicking the **Add All (>>)** button.

5. If you want to rename a field that you have added, click the
   **Rename Field** button, type a new name into the Rename
   field box, and then click **OK**.

**TIP**

> **Remove Unwanted Fields**    If you add a field that you
> don't want in the table, select the field in the **Fields in
> My New Table** list and click the **Remove (<)** button.
> To remove all the fields and start over, click **Remove
> All (<<)**.

6. Repeat steps 3 and 4 as needed to select more fields for the
   table. You can select fields from more than one of the sample
   tables for the table that you are creating (remember that you
   want fields in the table related only to a particular theme,
   such as customer information). When you're finished adding
   fields, click **Next** to continue.

7. The next screen asks you to provide a name for the table (see
   Figure 4.2). Type a more descriptive name if necessary to
   replace the default name.

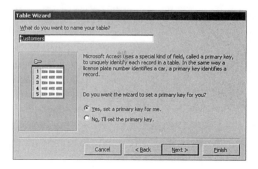

**FIGURE 4.2**
*Provide a name for the table and allow the wizard to select a primary key for the
table.*

**8.** This dialog box also asks whether you want the wizard to create a primary key for the table or allow you to select the primary key yourself. The *primary key* is the field that uniquely identifies each of the records in the table. For example, CustomerID is an excellent primary key because each customer is assigned a different ID number. In this case, click **Yes, Set a Primary Key for Me** to have the wizard choose your primary key field. You can learn to set your own primary keys in Lesson 5, "Creating a Table from Scratch."

**PLAIN ENGLISH**

**Primary Key**    The field that uniquely identifies each record in the table. Every table must have a primary key. This is usually an ID number because most other fields could conceivably hold the same data for more than one record (for example, you might have several people with the last name of Smith).

**9.** Click **Next** to continue. Because you're allowing the wizard to select the primary key, you are taken to the last wizard screen. On the last wizard screen, you have the options of modifying the table's design, entering data directly into the new table, or having the wizard create a data entry form for you. To see the table the wizard created, go with the default: Enter Data Directly into the Table (see Figure 4.3).

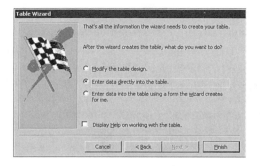

**FIGURE 4.3**
*After completing the table, you can have the wizard open it so that you can enter data.*

**10.** Click **Finish**.

The new table appears in the Access workspace (see Figure 4.4). From here you can enter data into the table, the specifics of which are discussed in Lesson 7, "Entering Data into a Table." When you close the table, it appears in the Object pane of the database window (you must also select the Tables object icon).

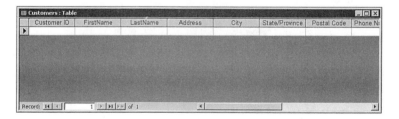

**FIGURE 4.4**
*Your new table appears in the Access workspace when you close the Table Wizard.*

In this lesson, you learned how to create a new table by using the Table Wizard. In the next lesson, you learn how to create a table in the design and datasheet views.

# LESSON 5
# Creating a Table from Scratch

*In this lesson, you learn how to create a table in the Table Design view and the Datasheet view.*

## CREATING TABLES WITHOUT THE WIZARD

Although the Table Wizard provides an easy method for quickly creating tables, it does not provide you with complete control over all the aspects of creating the table. It does allow you to select the fields used in the table from a set list, but it restricts you to only those predefined fields (there are also several types of fields, each used for a different data type). Creating tables from scratch in the Design view allows you to build the table from the bottom up and gives you complete control over all aspects of the table's design.

> **PLAIN ENGLISH**
>
> **Design View**   This view allows you to enter field names, select the data type that a field will hold, and customize each field's properties. A Design view is available for all the Access objects, including tables, forms, queries, and reports.

The Design view isn't the only way to create a table from scratch in Access. You can also create a table in the Datasheet view by labeling your field columns directly on the table's datasheet, which is similar to creating a worksheet in Excel. Take a look at both methods for creating a new table.

**TIP**

> **Datasheet View**    This view places each record in a separate row and each field in a separate column (column headings are provided by the field names). This view is used to enter data directly into the table. You will use the Datasheet view whenever you want to view the records in the table or add or edit records.

## CREATING A TABLE IN TABLE DESIGN VIEW

When you create a table in the Design view, you are creating the structure for the table; you create a list of the fields that will be in the table. You also select the data type for each field. (Fields can hold text, numbers, even graphics—you learn the types of fields that can be created later in this lesson.) You also have the option of entering a description for each field. Field descriptions are useful in that they provide a quick summary of the type of data that goes into the field.

Another issue that relates to creating a table in the Design view (or editing a table's structure in the Design view) is that any changes you make must be saved before closing the table. If you have worked in other applications, such as Word or Excel, you might think that saving your work is just common sense. However, when you actually start working on entering data into a table or a form, Access automatically saves your records as you enter them. Therefore, in Access, you need to remember to save only the changes that you make to the structure of a table, form, query, or report. You learn more about this in Lesson 6, "Editing a Table's Structure."

**TIP**

> **Field Naming Rules**    Field names in Access can be up to 64 characters long and can contain spaces and both alphanumeric and numeric characters. You can't use periods or exclamation points in your field names. Also, avoid special characters (such as $, %, or #) in field names because some of these characters have special meanings in Access code.

To create a table in Table Design view, follow these steps:

1. In the database window (of a particular database) click the
   **Tables** icon if necessary, and then double-click **Create Table in
   Design View**. The Table Design view opens (see Figure 5.1).

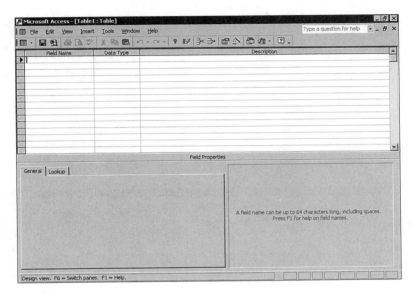

**FIGURE 5.1**
*The Table Design view allows you to create the structure for your table.*

2. Be sure that the insertion point is in the first row of the Field
   Name column. Type the field name for the first field in your
   table. Then, press **Tab** or **Enter** to move to the Data Type
   column.

3. When you move to the Data Type column, an arrow appears
   for a drop-down list. The default data type setting is Text;
   several other data types are available, such as AutoNumber,
   which automatically numbers each of your records. This field
   type is excellent for customer number fields or employee ID
   fields. Click the **Data Type** drop-down list and select a field

type. The different data types are discussed later in this lesson, in the section "Understanding Data Types and Formats."

4. After selecting the data type, press **Enter** to move to the Description column; type a description for the field. (This is optional; the table will work fine without it.)

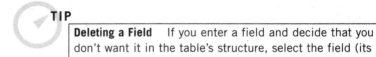

**TIP**

> **Deleting a Field**   If you enter a field and decide that you don't want it in the table's structure, select the field (its entire row) and press the **Delete** key.

5. Enter other fields and their field types (descriptions are optional) as needed. Figure 5.2 shows the structure for a table that will be used to enter product information.

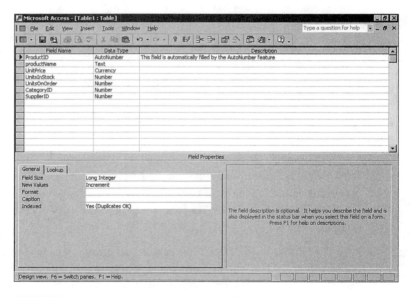

**FIGURE 5.2**
*A table's structure consists of several fields; fields may differ by field type.*

## SETTING THE PRIMARY KEY

An important aspect of table structure design is that each table must have a field that is used to uniquely identify the records in the table. This field is called the *primary key*. Setting an appropriate key is trickier than it appears because no two records can have the same key value. In a table of customers, for example, you might think the Last Name field would be a good key, but this theory falls flat as soon as you find that you have more than one customer with the same last name. A more appropriate primary key for your customers is a Social Security number (although people don't like to give these out) because it uniquely identifies each customer.

A good general rule is to create an identification field, such as a customer number, that allows you to assign a sequential number to each customer as you add them to your database table. Access can even help you out with the assigning of numbers to the customers because you can make the field type for the Customer Number field AutoNumber. An AutoNumber field type assigns a number to each record starting with the number 1.

**TIP**

**Creating the Primary Key**     Typically, the first field in the table serves as the primary key.

To set a primary key, follow these steps:

1.  In Table Design view, select the field that you want for the primary key.

2.  Select **Edit, Primary Key**, or click the **Primary Key** button on the toolbar. A key symbol appears to the left of the field name, as shown in Figure 5.3.

Primary Key

| Field Name | Data Type | Description |
|---|---|---|
| ProductID | AutoNumber | This field is automatically filled by the AutoNumber feature |
| productName | Text | |
| UnitPrice | Currency | |
| UnitsInStock | Number | |
| UnitsOnOrder | Number | |
| CategoryID | Number | |
| SupplierID | Number | |

**FIGURE 5.3**
*The primary key field is marked by a key symbol.*

3. After you select the primary key and have finished entering your table fields, you should save the table. Click the **Save** button on the Table Design toolbar to open the Save As dialog box.

4. Enter a name for the table, and then click **OK**.

5. After saving the table, you can either switch to the Datasheet view (to enter data) by clicking the **View** button on the tool-bar, or you can choose to close the table by clicking the table's **Close** (x) button.

**PLAIN ENGLISH**

**No Primary Key!**    If you attempt to close your new table in the Design view without specifying a primary key (even if you have saved the table), a message appears, letting you know that no primary key has been assigned. Click **Yes** on the message box to have Access assign a primary key to the table. If you have set up your table to contain an AutoNumber field, Access will make this field the primary key. Otherwise, Access creates a new AutoNumber field in the table and specifies it as the primary key. You can change the name of this new field as needed.

## UNDERSTANDING DATA TYPES AND FORMATS

To assign appropriate data types to the fields you create in a table, it is necessary for you to know what differentiates the different data types available for use with your table fields. When you create a field, you want to assign it a data type so that Access knows how to handle its contents. The following are the different data types you can choose:

- **Text**—Text and numbers up to 255 characters (numbers that are not going to be used in calculations).

- **Memo**—Lengthy text.

- **Number**—Numbers used in mathematical calculations.

- **Date/Time**—Date and time values.

- **Currency**—Numbers formatted for currency.

- **AutoNumber**—Sequentially numbers each new record. Only one AutoNumber field can be placed in a table. This field type is typically used for the primary key field.

- **Yes/No**—Lets you set up fields with a true/false data type.

- **OLE (Object Linking and Embedding)**—A picture, spreadsheet, or other item from another software program.

- **Hyperlink**—A link to another file or a location on a Web page. This field type lets you jump from the current field to information in another file.

- **Lookup Wizard**—This field type chooses its values from another table.

In addition to a field type, each field has other formatting options you can set. They appear in the bottom half of the dialog box, in the Field Properties area. The formatting options change depending on the field type; there are too many to list here, but Table 5.1 shows some of the most important ones you'll encounter.

**TABLE 5.1**　Formatting Options for Data Types

| Formatting Option | Description |
| --- | --- |
| Field Size | The maximum number of characters a user can input in that field (applies only to text fields). |
| Format | A drop-down list of the available formats for that field type. You can also create custom formats. |
| Decimal Places | For number fields, you can set the default number of decimal places that a number shows. |
| Default Value | If a field is usually going to contain a certain value (for example, a certain ZIP code for almost everyone), you can set that as the Default Value option. It always appears in a new record, but you can type over it in the rare instances when it doesn't apply. |
| Required | Choose **Yes** if a particular field is required to be filled in each record. |

The best general rule for setting the data type for the field is to take a moment to consider what kind of data will go into that field. For example, if you are working with the monetary value of a product, you will probably want to use currency.

The different formatting options provided for a field in the Field Properties box are often used to help make sure that data is entered correctly. For example, the Field Size option can be used to limit a Number data type field to only a single or double digit. In the case of the default value, you can actually save data entry time because you use this option when a particular field almost always has a certain value or text entry.

## CREATING A TABLE IN THE DATASHEET VIEW

After you feel comfortable creating new tables in the Design view, you might want to dive right in and create tables in the Datasheet view. Creating tables this way immediately creates a table with 20 field columns and 30 record rows. This method still requires, however, that you enter the Table Design view to specify the key field, the field data types, field descriptions, and any field property changes.

Creating tables in the Datasheet view is really useful only if you feel the need to quickly enter some data into the table before setting up the table's properties. To create a table in the Datasheet view, follow these steps:

1. In the database window (with the Table icon selected), double-click **Create Table by Entering Data**. A new table in Datasheet view appears in the Access workspace (see Figure 5.4).

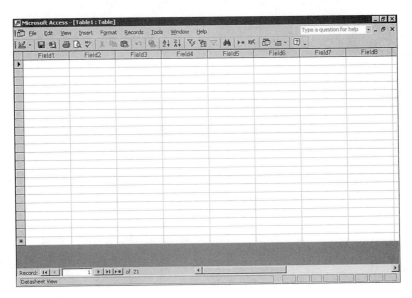

**FIGURE 5.4**
*Tables can be created in the Datasheet view.*

2. To enter the field names, double-click any field column heading (Field1, Field2, and so on). Then, type in the field name.

3. After you have placed the field names, you can begin entering data.

Creating a table in the Datasheet view might be fine for quickly entering data, but you will still probably need to switch to the Table Design view at some point and set up the various field data types and properties.

 You can switch to the Design view from the Datasheet view by clicking the **View** icon on the Table Datasheet toolbar. Remember to save any changes to the table's design that you make in the Design view.

In this lesson, you learned to create a table in the Design view and the Datasheet view. You also learned about the different field data types. In the next lesson, you learn how to edit and enhance your table's structure.

# LESSON 6
# Editing a Table's Structure

*In this lesson, you learn how to change your table structure by adding and removing fields and hiding columns.*

## EDITING FIELDS AND THEIR PROPERTIES

After you've created a table with the Table Wizard or from scratch, you might find that you want to fine-tune the table's structure. This requires that you edit your fields and their properties.

You can delete fields, add new fields, or change the order of fields in the table. You also can change a field's data type. Because the table's structure is discussed here and not the data, you need to work in the Table Design view.

> **CAUTION**
>
> **Get the Table's Structure Down Before Entering Data** You should try to finalize the table's field structure and properties before you enter data. Changing data types or other field properties can actually delete data that you've already entered into the table.

You can open an existing table in the Table Design view in several ways:

- In the database window, click the **Table** object icon, select the table you want to work with in the right pane of the database window, and then click the **Design** button on the database window's toolbar.

- Right-click the table in the database window and select **Design View** from the shortcut menu that appears.

- If you are in the table's Datasheet view, click the **View** button on the Table Datasheet view toolbar.

## CHANGING FIELD NAMES AND DATA TYPES

When you are in the Design view (see Figure 6.1), you can enhance or rework your table's structure. For example, you can change a field's name. Just double-click the field's current name and type in a new one.

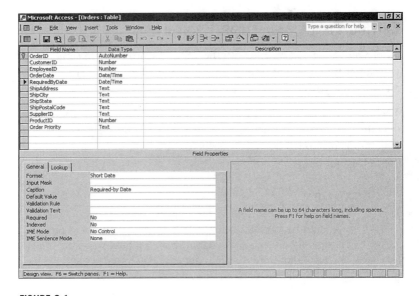

**FIGURE 6.1**
*A table's existing structure can be edited in the Design view.*

You can also change the data type for an existing field. Click the field's Data Type box and select a new data type from the drop-down list. Remember that when you change a field name or a field's data type, you must save the changes that you've made to the table's structure.

## SETTING FIELD PROPERTIES

Field properties can also be edited for each field using the various Properties boxes found in the Field Properties pane. Lesson 5, "Creating a Table from Scratch," provides a quick overview of some of the properties that are available.

Another very useful field property, particularly for fields that use text entries (remember that text entries can include numbers) is an *input mask*. An input mask is used to format that data as you enter it into a field. For example, you might want to enter a date in a particular format, such as the format xx/xx/xx. The input mask can be used so that when you enter the data into the date field, all you need to enter is the two-digit input for the month, day, and year. Access automatically places the slashes in the field for you.

### PLAIN ENGLISH

**Input Mask**   A field property that limits the number of characters that can be entered in a field.

Input masks are also very useful for entering ZIP codes. The input mask limits the number of characters that can be entered (such as those in a ZIP code), and if you use the 5-4 ZIP code format, the input mask can place the dash into the ZIP code for you.

To create an input mask for a field (such as a date field or a Design view field), follow these steps:

1. Click in the Field Name box to select the field for which you want to create the input mask.

2. In the Field Properties pane, click in the Input Mask box. The Input Mask Wizard button appears in the box.

3. Click the **Input Mask Wizard** button to open the dialog box shown in Figure 6.2.

**FIGURE 6.2**
*The Input Mask Wizard helps you create an input mask for a field.*

4. The Input Mask Wizard offers a list of possible masks for the field based on the field's data type. For example, Figure 6.2 shows the Input Mask Wizard used for a field with the Date data type. Select one of the mask formats listed, and then click **Next**.

5. The next wizard screen shows you the input mask you have chosen and gives you the opportunity to change the format. You can also test the input mask format by typing some data into the Try It box. Edit the input mask format if necessary and then click **Next** to continue.

6. You are taken to the last wizard screen. Click **Finish** to create the input mask. The input mask appears in the Input Mask box in the Field Properties pane (see Figure 6.3).

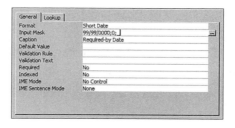

**FIGURE 6.3**
*The input mask appears in the Input Mask box.*

7. Click the **Save** button to save changes that you have made to the table structure.

## ADDING, DELETING, AND MOVING FIELDS

You can also add additional fields to your table's structure. All you have to do is add a new row to the field list and then enter the new field name and data type. Follow these steps:

1. Click the record selector (the gray square to the left of the field name) to select the field that will follow the new field that you create (in the field list).

2. Select **Insert, Row**. A blank row appears in the Field Name list.

3. Enter a name, a data type, a description, and so on for the new field.

You can also delete any unwanted fields. Click the record selector for the field and then press the **Delete** key on the keyboard. A message box appears that requires you to confirm the field's deletion. Click **Yes** to delete the field.

**CAUTION**

**Don't Remove Important Fields!**    Be very careful about deleting fields after you start entering records into your table. When you delete a field, all the information stored for each record in that field is gone, too. The best time to experiment with deleting fields is before you enter any data into the table.

You can also rearrange the fields in the table. Click the record selector for the field to select the field. Then, use the mouse to drag the field to a new position in the field list. Remember to save any changes that you have made to the table's structure.

## DELETING A TABLE

No matter how hard you work on a table's design, you might find as
you design the other tables for your database that you just don't need
a particular table. It's easy to delete a table (although it might not
be easy to forget the time that you spent creating the table); simply
follow these steps:

1. In the database window, click the **Tables** object type.

2. In the right pane of the database window, select the table you
   want to delete.

3. Select **Edit**, **Delete**, or press the **Delete** key on your keyboard.

4. A message appears asking whether you're sure you want to
   do this. Click **Yes**.

In this lesson, you learned how to modify your table's properties in
the Design View. You also learned how to create an input mask for a
field. Adding and removing fields was also covered. In the next lesson,
you learn how to enter data into the table in the Datasheet view and
navigate the table.

# LESSON 7
# Entering Data into a Table

*In this lesson, you learn how to add records to a table, print the table, and close it.*

## ENTERING A RECORD

After you've created the table and fine-tuned its structure, you are ready to enter data into the table. This means that you should have access to all the data that you need to enter. Then, all you have to do is open the table and input the data records.

> **TIP**
>
> **Using Forms to Enter Data**  Access doesn't limit you to entering data directly into the table. You can also enter data using a form. Form creation and data entry using a form are covered in Lesson 13, "Modifying a Form."

First, from the database window, double-click the table in which you want to enter the records. The table opens in the Datasheet view (see Figure 7.1). If this is the first time you have entered data into the table, only one empty record appears in the table. As you complete each record, a new blank record (a new row) appears.

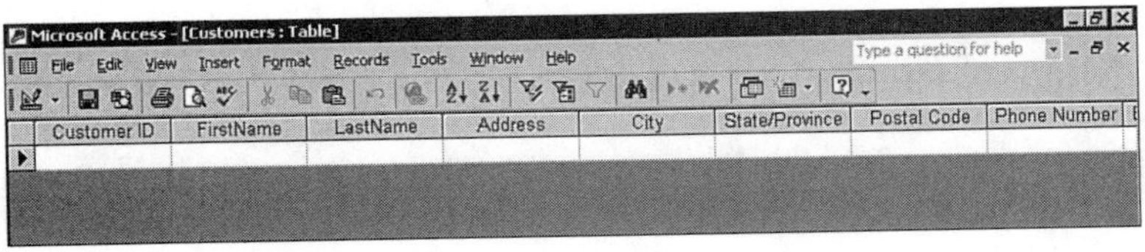

**FIGURE 7.1**
*A table's existing structure can be edited in the Design view.*

To enter records into the table, follow these steps:

1. Click in the first field of the first blank record (if necessary). If the first field is an identification field, such as Customer ID, and you selected the AutoNumber data type for the field, press **Tab** to advance to the next field (the AutoNumber field is automatically filled in for you).

2. Type the value for that field.

3. Press **Tab** to move to the next field and enter that field's data.

4. Continue pressing **Tab** and entering data until you complete the last field in the record. When you press **Tab** in the last field, a new record (a new row) appears, and the insertion point moves to the first field in the new record.

5. Continue entering records as required.

**TIP**

> **Data Entry Tricks**    Access offers some hotkey combinations for entering dates and data found in the same field in a previous record. To insert the current date, press **Ctrl+;** (semicolon). To insert the current time, press **Ctrl+:** (colon). To repeat the value from the same field in the previous record, press **Ctrl+'** (apostrophe).

You should be aware that, as you enter each field's data and move onto the next field, Access automatically saves your table data. This is very different from other Office applications, such as Word or Excel, where you must save your data after entering it.

## MOVING AROUND IN A TABLE

So far, you've used the Tab key only to move from field to field in the table. You might have also used the mouse to move the insertion point from a field in one record to another field in that record, or to a field in a different record. Because you do your data entry from the keyboard, Access provides several keystrokes that can be used to navigate the various fields in the table. For example, you can back up one field in a record by pressing **Shift+Tab**. Table 7.1 summarizes the various keyboard shortcuts for moving around in a table.

**TABLE 7.1**    Table Movement Keys

| To Move To | Press |
|---|---|
| Next field | Tab |
| Previous field | Shift+Tab |
| Last field in the record | End |
| First field in the record | Home |
| Same field in the next record | Down-arrow key |
| Same field in the previous record | Up-arrow key |
| Same field in the last record | Ctrl+down-arrow key |
| Same field in the first record | Ctrl+up-arrow key |
| Last field in the last record | Ctrl+End |
| First field in the first record | Ctrl+Home |

## HIDING A FIELD

When you are entering data into the table, you might find that you have not actually collected the data that you need to enter into a particular field. This means that you must skip this field in all the records as you enter your data (until you come up with the data).

You can hide a field or fields in the table datasheet. This doesn't delete the field column or disrupt any of the field properties that you set for that particular field. It just hides the field from your view as you enter your data. To hide a field, follow these steps:

1. In the Datasheet view, select the field or fields that you want to hide (click a field's column heading, as shown in Figure 7.2). To select multiple contiguous fields, click the first field, and then hold down the **Shift** key and click the last field.

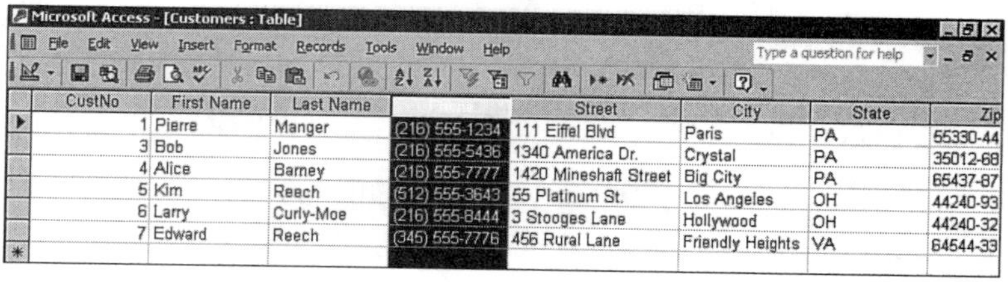

**FIGURE 7.2**
*You can select a column and then hide it.*

2. Select **Format** and then **Hide Columns**, or right-click the column and select **Hide Columns**. The column or columns disappear.

3. Enter your data records into your table; the hidden column is skipped as you move from column to column.

4. When you have finished entering data into the other fields in the table, you can unhide the column. Select **Format, Unhide Columns**. The Unhide Columns dialog box appears (see Figure 7.3). Fields with a check mark next to them are unhidden; fields without a check mark are hidden.

5. Click the check box of any hidden field to "unhide" the field.

6. Click **Close**. The hidden column (or columns) reappear in the table.

**FIGURE 7.3**
*The Unhide Columns dialog box shows you which columns are currently hidden.*

## FREEZING A COLUMN

Another useful manipulation of the field columns in an Access table that can make data entry easier is freezing a column. For example, if a table has a large number of fields, as you move to the right in the table during data entry, fields in the beginning of the table scroll off the screen. This can be very annoying if you lose your place, because you might not remember for which customer you were entering data.

You can freeze columns so that they remain on the screen even when you scroll to the far right of a table record. Follow these steps:

1. Click the column heading of the field column you want to freeze. This selects the entire column of data.

2. Click the **Format** menu; then click **Freeze Columns**.

3. The frozen field column moves over to the first field position in the table. Click anywhere in the table to deselect the field column.

4. When you move through the fields in a record toward the far right of the table, the frozen field column remains on the screen. This allows you to see important data such as the customer's name as you attempt to enter other data into a particular record.

You can freeze multiple columns if you want, such as the Last Name field and the First Name field. When you want to unfreeze the column or columns in the table, select the **Format** menu, and then select **Unfreeze All Columns**.

## USING THE SPELLING FEATURE

To ensure your data entry accuracy, you can quickly check the spelling of the data that you have input into your table. This should help you clear up any typos that might have happened during your entry of the table records.

The Spelling feature, obviously, won't be able to check the numerical information that you input or help you enter proper names, but it can help you avoid embarrassing misspellings. To check the spelling in a table, follow these steps:

1. Click the **Spelling** button on the Table Datasheet toolbar, or you can select **Tools, Spelling** to open the Spelling dialog box (see Figure 7.4).

**FIGURE 7.4**
*The Spelling feature enables you to quickly check for typos and misspellings in your Access table.*

2. Words flagged as misspelled appear in the dialog box. A list of suggestions also appears from which you can choose a correct spelling. You can either correct the misspellings manually or click one of the suggestions. When you're ready,

click **Change** to correct the spelling. The Speller then moves
to the next misspelled word.

3. If you want to add the flagged word to the dictionary, click
   the **Add** button. If a flagged word is correctly spelled, click
   the **Ignore** button to ignore the word and continue with the
   spell check.

4. If the field containing the flagged word is a field that typically holds proper names or other values that the Spelling
   feature will always flag as misspelled, click the **Ignore
   "Field Name"** button.

## CLOSING A TABLE

After you have finished entering data into a particular table and check-
ing the spelling, you should close that table. Because the table is just
like any other window, click the table's **Close (x)** button to close the
table. You are then returned to the database window.

In this lesson, you learned how to enter records into a table, navigate
the table from the keyboard, and hide columns in the table. You also
learned to check the spelling in the table and close the table. In the
next lesson, you learn how to edit data in a table.

# LESSON 8
# Editing Data in a Table

*In this lesson, you learn how to edit information in a field, select records, and insert and delete records.*

## CHANGING A FIELD'S CONTENT

After you enter the records in a table, you will probably find that you need to make some changes; sometimes data is entered incorrectly or the data for a particular record might actually change. Editing a field's content is easy. You can replace the old field content entirely or edit it.

## REPLACING A FIELD'S CONTENT

If the data in a field must be updated or has been entered incorrectly, the easiest way to replace this data is to enter the new data from scratch. To replace the old content in a field, follow these steps:

1. You can use the **Tab** key to move to the field you want to edit (the contents of the field will be selected), or select the contents of a field with the mouse. To use your mouse, place the mouse pointer on the upper-left or right edge of the field. The mouse pointer becomes a plus sign (+) as shown in Figure 8.1. Click the field to select its content.

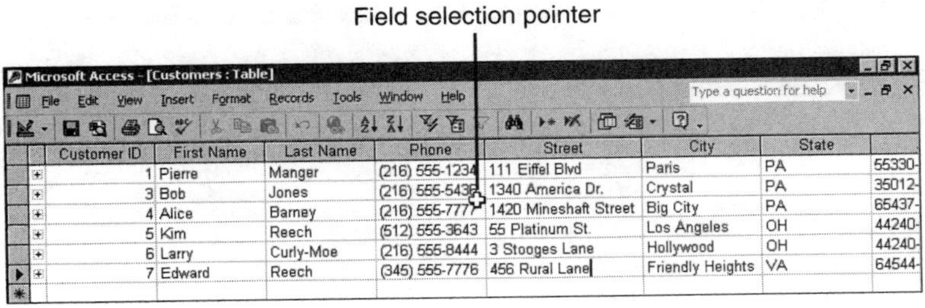

Field selection pointer

**FIGURE 8.1**
To select a field's entire contents, make sure that the mouse pointer is a plus sign when you click.

2. Type the new data, which replaces the old data.

3. You can the use the **Tab** key or the mouse to move to the next field you need to edit.

## EDITING A FIELD'S CONTENT WITH A MOUSE

Replacing the entire contents of a field is kind of a heavy-handed way to edit a field if you need to correct the entry of only one or two characters. You can also fine-tune your entries by editing a portion of the data in the field. Follow these steps:

1. Place the mouse pointer over the position in the field where you want to correct data. The mouse pointer should become an I-beam.

2. Click once to place the insertion point at that position in the field (see Figure 8.2). Now you can edit the content of the field.

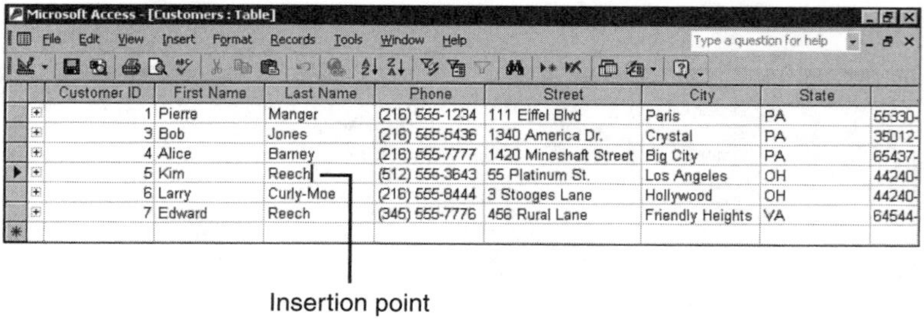

Insertion point

**FIGURE 8.2**
*Place the insertion point into a field to edit its content.*

3. Press **Backspace** to remove the character to the left of the insertion point or **Delete** to remove the character to the right of the insertion point.

4. Enter new text into the field as needed. New entries in the field are inserted, meaning they displace the current entry but do not overwrite it.

## MOVING AROUND A FIELD WITH A KEYBOARD

Although the mouse provides a quick way to place the insertion point into a field, you might want to be able to navigate inside a field using the keyboard, especially when you are editing a fairly long field entry. Access provides several keyboard possibilities for moving inside a cell. Table 8.1 lists these keyboard-movement keys.

**TABLE 8.1** Moving Within a Field

| To Move | Press |
| --- | --- |
| One character to the right | Right-arrow key |
| One character to the left | Left-arrow key |
| One word to the right | Ctrl+right-arrow key |
| One word to the left | Ctrl+left-arrow key |

| To Move | Press |
|---------|-------|
| To the end of the line | End |
| To the beginning of the line | Home |

## Moving and Copying Data

As in any Office application, you can use the Cut, Copy, and Paste commands to copy and move data in your table fields. This is particularly useful if you want to quickly copy a ZIP code that is the same for more than one customer, or you want to cut data that you put in the wrong field, so that you can paste it into the appropriate field. To use copy, cut, and paste, follow these steps:

1. Select the entire field or the portion of a field's content that you want to cut or copy.

2. Select **Edit**, and then **Cut** (to move) or **Copy** (to copy). Or press **Ctrl+X** to cut or **Ctrl+C** to copy.

3. Position the insertion point where you want to insert the cut or copied material.

4. Select **Edit, Paste,** or press **Ctrl+V** to paste.

**TIP**

 **Toolbar Shortcuts**    You can also use the Cut, Copy, and Paste buttons on the Table Datasheet toolbar to manipulate text in the table fields.

## Inserting and Deleting Fields

You can also insert and delete fields in the Table Datasheet view. This allows you to quickly enter the data into a new field or delete an unneeded field. It is preferable, however, to insert new fields into the table in the Design view and then enter data. This is because you will eventually have to switch to Table Design view to specify the data type or other properties of the new field.

To insert a field, follow these steps:

1. Select the existing field column in which you want to insert the new field. The new field column is inserted to the left of the currently selected field column.

2. Select **Insert, Column**. The new column appears in the table (see Figure 8.3).

| Customer ID | FirstName | LastName | Phone | Address | City | State | Field1 | |
|---|---|---|---|---|---|---|---|---|
| 1 | Pierre | Manger | (216) 555-1234 | 111 Eiffel Blvd | Paris | PA | | 5 |
| 2 | Bob | Jones | (216) 555-5436 | 1340 America C | Crystal | PA | | 3 |
| 3 | Alice | Barney | (216) 555-7777 | 1420 Mineshaft | Big City | PA | | 8 |
| 4 | Kim | Reech | (512) 555-3643 | 55 Platinum St. | Los Angeles | OH | | 4 |
| 5 | Larry | Curly-Moe | (216) 555-8444 | 3 Stooges Lane | Hollywood | OH | | 4 |
| 6 | Edward | Reech | (345) 555-7776 | 456 Rural Lane | Friendly Heights | VA | | 8 |

**FIGURE 8.3**
*New field columns can be added to the table in the Datasheet view.*

3. To name the new field, double-click the field heading (such as Field1) and type the new name for the field.

4. Enter data into the new field as needed.

Deleting a field or fields is also very straightforward. Remember, however, that deleting a field also deletes any data that you have entered into that field. Select the field that you want to delete and then select **Edit, Delete Column**. You are asked to verify the deletion of the field. If you're sure, click **Yes**.

## INSERTING NEW RECORDS

As your customer base increases or other new data becomes available for your database, you will definitely be adding records to the various tables in the database. New records are inserted automatically. As soon as you begin to enter data into a record, a new blank record appears at the bottom of the table (see Figure 8.4).

| Customer ID | FirstName | LastName | Phone | Address | City | State | Zip |
|---|---|---|---|---|---|---|---|
| 1 | Pierre | Manger | (216) 555-1234 | 111 Eiffel Blvd | Paris | PA | 55330-4433 |
| 2 | Bob | Jones | (216) 555-5436 | 1340 America C | Crystal | PA | 35012-6894 |
| 3 | Alice | Barney | (216) 555-7777 | 1420 Mineshaft | Big City | PA | 65437-8765 |
| 4 | Kim | Reech | (512) 555-3643 | 55 Platinum St. | Los Angeles | OH | 44240-9354 |
| 5 | Larry | Curly-Moe | (216) 555-8444 | 3 Stooges Lane | Hollywood | OH | 44240-3210 |
| 6 | Edward | Reech | (345) 555-7776 | 456 Rural Lane | Friendly Heights | VA | 64544-3343 |

New record

**FIGURE 8.4**
*New records are automatically inserted at the bottom of the table.*

This process is re-created every time you complete a record and then start a new record. Inserting information into the first field of the new record inserts another new record below the one on which you are working.

You can't insert new records between existing ones or at the top of the table. New records are always entered at the bottom of the table, below the last completed record.

**TIP**

> **What If I Want the Records in a Different Order?** Although you can enter new records only at the bottom of the table, you can rearrange the order of your records if you want. This can be done using the sorting feature discussed in Lesson 17, "Creating a Simple Query."

## DELETING RECORDS

You will probably find that certain records in the table become outdated or no longer pertinent to the database (such as an employee who has left your company but still has a record in the Employee table). You can delete a record or several records at a time.

To delete a record or records, follow these steps:

1. To select the record that you want to delete, click the record selector button (the small gray box to the left of the record, as shown in Figure 8.5). If you want to select multiple records, click and drag the record selector buttons of the contiguous records.

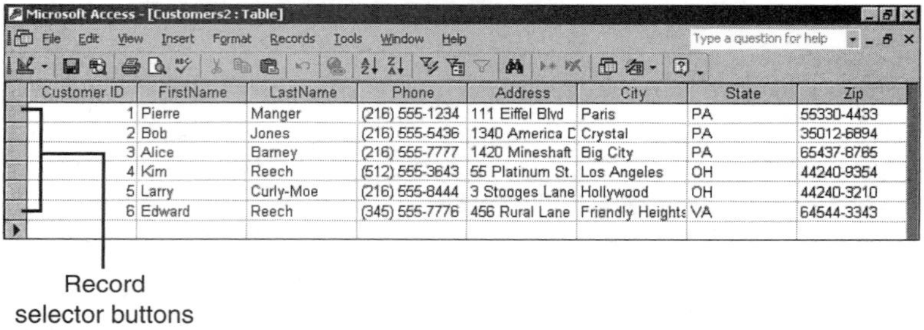
Microsoft Access - [Customers2 : Table]
File Edit View Insert Format Records Tools Window Help
Type a question for help
Customer ID FirstName LastName Phone Address City State Zip
1 Pierre Manger (216) 555-1234 111 Eiffel Blvd Paris PA 55330-4433
2 Bob Jones (216) 555-5436 1340 America D Crystal PA 35012-6894
3 Alice Barney (216) 555-7777 1420 Mineshaft Big City PA 65437-8765
4 Kim Reech (512) 555-3643 55 Platinum St. Los Angeles OH 44240-9354
5 Larry Curly-Moe (216) 555-8444 3 Stooges Lane Hollywood OH 44240-3210
6 Edward Reech (345) 555-7776 456 Rural Lane Friendly Heights VA 64544-3343
Record selector buttons

**FIGURE 8.5**
*Select the record or records you want to delete.*

2. To delete the record or records, perform any of the following:
   - Click the **Delete Record** button on the toolbar.
   - Press the **Delete** key on the keyboard.
   - Select the **Edit**, **Delete Record**.
3. A dialog box appears, letting you know that you are deleting a record and will not be able to undo this action. To delete the record or records, click **Yes**.

**CAUTION**

**Deleting Records Affects the AutoNumber Sequence**
When you delete records in the table that were assigned an identification number using the AutoNumber data type, that number (or numbers) will be lost from the sequence. For example, if you delete a customer with

the AutoNumber customer ID of 3, the number 3 is removed from the sequence. When listing your customers, the customer numbers would then appear as 1, 2, 4, 5, and so on.

In this lesson, you learned how to edit data in a field, how to insert and delete fields, and how to copy and move data from place to place. You also learned how to insert and delete records in the table. In the next lesson, you learn how to format your table.

# LESSON 9

# Formatting Access Tables

*In this lesson, you learn how to improve the look of a table by adjusting the row and column sizes, changing the font, and choosing text alignment options.*

## CHANGING THE LOOK OF YOUR TABLE

Most people don't spend a lot of time formatting Access tables because they don't always use the table for data entry; instead, they use a form. Most people also don't typically print their tables. They use data-entry forms to see the records onscreen and reports to print their records. The tables are merely holding tanks for the raw data.

However, creating forms and reports might be more work than you want to tackle right now. And formatting a table so that data entry is a little less tedious (and less hard on the eyes) or so you can quickly print a copy of a table (covered in Lesson 22, "Printing Access Objects") is certainly no crime. Making a table more readable onscreen is certainly nice for the person using the table to enter data.

## CHANGING COLUMN WIDTH AND ROW HEIGHT

One common problem with a table is that you can't see the complete contents of the fields. Fields often hold more data than will fit across a column's width. This causes the data in your table to appear to be cut off.

You can fix this problem in two ways: make the column wider so it can display more data, or make the row taller so it can display more than one line of data.

## CHANGING COLUMN WIDTH

Access offers many ways to adjust column width in a table; you can choose the method you like best. One of the easiest ways to adjust the column width is to drag the column headings. Follow these steps:

1. Position the mouse pointer between two field names (column headings) so that the pointer turns into a vertical line with left- and right-pointing arrows; this is the sizing tool (see Figure 9.1). You'll be adjusting the column on the left; the column on the right will move to accommodate it.

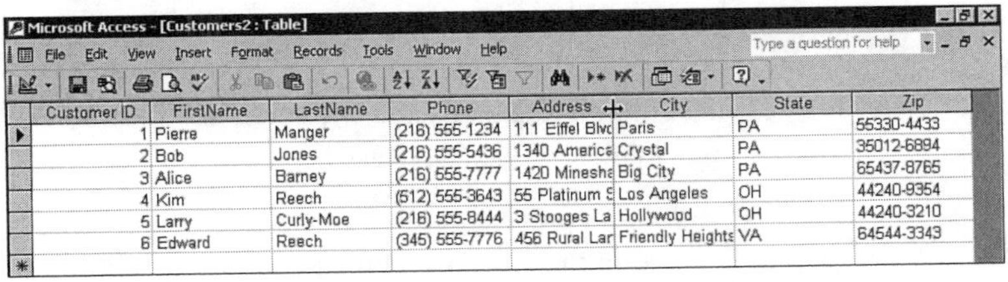

**FIGURE 9.1**
*Position the mouse pointer between two column headings.*

2. Click and hold the mouse button and drag the edge of the column to the right or left to increase or decrease the width.

3. Release the mouse button when the column is the desired width.

Alternatively, you can double-click the column's vertical border when the sizing tool is showing, which automatically adjusts the width of the column on the left so that it accommodates the largest amount of data entered in that particular field.

Another, more precise, way to adjust column width is to use the Column Width dialog box. Follow these steps:

1. Select the column(s) for which you want to adjust the width.

2. From the **Format** menu, choose **Column Width**, or right-click and choose **Column Width** from the shortcut menu. The Column Width dialog box appears (see Figure 9.2).

**FIGURE 9.2**
*Adjust the column width precisely in the Column Width dialog box.*

3. Do one of the following to set the column width:

   • Adjust the column to exactly the width needed for the longest entry in it by clicking **Best Fit**.

   • Set the width to a precise number of field characters by typing a value in the **Column Width** text box.

   • Reset the column width to its default value by selecting the **Standard Width** check box.

4. Click **OK** to apply the changes.

Because changing the width of a field column in the table is actually changing the field's length (which you designated in the Design view when you created the table), you do need to save these changes. Click the **Save** button on the Table Datasheet toolbar.

## CHANGING ROW HEIGHT

You can also change the height of the rows or records in the table. This allows you to see more text in a field that contains a large amount of data, such as a memo field.

**CAUTION**

**Adjusting One Row Height Adjusts Them All**   If you change the height of one row, it changes the height of all the rows or records in the table. Edit the row height only in cases where it allows you to see more data in a particular field for each record.

One way to make rows taller (or shorter) is to drag a particular row's border, enlarging the record's row. Position the mouse pointer between two rows in the row selection area, and then drag up or down. Remember that this changes the height of all the rows in the table (meaning all the records).

Another way is to use the Row Height dialog box. It works the same as the Column Width dialog box, except that no Best Fit option is available. Select the **Format** menu and then choose **Row Height**. The Row Height dialog box appears.

Enter the height for the table's rows into the dialog box (or click **Standard Height** to return the rows to the default height) and click **OK**.

## CHANGING THE FONT AND FONT SIZE

Unlike other Access views (such as Report and Form), you can't format individual fields or portions of the data that are entered in a particular view. You can format the font style only for the entire table. Font changes are automatically applied to all data in the table, including the field column headings.

Font changes that you make in Datasheet view won't affect the way your data looks in other Access objects, such as your reports, queries, or forms. They affect only the table itself.

There are some good reasons for changing the font style in a table. For example, you might want to increase the font size so that the field contents are easier to read. Or you might bold the data in the table so that you get a nice, crisp printout when you print the table (see Lesson 22).

## CHANGING THE DEFAULT FONT STYLE

If the default style used in Access for tables has been bugging you from the beginning, you can change the default font used in Datasheet view for all the tables you create in Access.

Select **Tools**, and then **Options**. Select the **Datasheet** tab of the Options dialog box (see Figure 9.3).

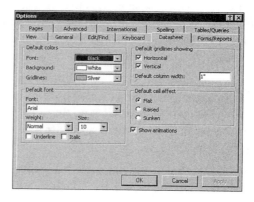

**FIGURE 9.3**
*You can change the default Datasheet font properties in the Options dialog box.*

Use the different drop-down menus in the Default Font box of the Datasheet tab to select the font name, font weight, or font size. When you have finished making your changes, click **OK**.

## CHANGING THE FONT STYLE FOR A TABLE

Font changes that you make to a specific table override the default font settings. To choose a different font for a currently open table datasheet, follow these steps:

1. From the **Format** menu, choose **Font**. The Font dialog box appears (see Figure 9.4).

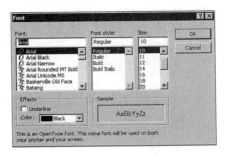

**FIGURE 9.4**
*Select the different font options in the Font dialog box.*

2. Select a font from the **Font** list box.

3. Select a style from the **Font Style** list box.

4. Select a size from the **Size** list box.

5. Select a color from the **Color** drop-down list.

6. (Optional) Click the **Underline** check box if you want under-lined text.

7. You can see a sample of your changes in the Sample area. When you're happy with the look of the sample text, click **OK**.

Another way you can change the look of your table is with the Datasheet Formatting dialog box (choose **Format, Datasheet**). You can change the cell special effects, background color, the color of the grid lines between each row and column, and whether the lines show.

In this lesson, you learned how to format column widths and table heights. You also worked with changing the font attributes for a table. In the next lesson, you learn how to get help in Access.

# LESSON 10

# Getting Help in Microsoft Access

*In this lesson, you learn how to access and use the Help system in Microsoft Access.*

## HELP: WHAT'S AVAILABLE?

Microsoft Access supplies a Help system that makes it easy for you to look up information on Access commands and features as you create database tables and other objects and enter information into your database. Because every person is different, the Help system can be accessed in several ways. You can

- Ask a question in the Ask a Question box.

- Ask the Office Assistant for help.

- Get help on a particular element you see onscreen with the What's This? tool.

- Use the Contents, Answer Wizard, and Index tabs in the Help window to get help.

- Access the Office on the Web feature to view Web pages containing help information (if you are connected to the Internet).

## USING THE ASK A QUESTION BOX

The Ask a Question box is a new way to quickly open the Access Help system. The Ask a Question box resides at the top right of the Access application window.

For example, if you are working in Access and wish to view information on how to create a new table, type **How do I create a table?** into the Ask a Question box. Then press the **Enter** key. A shortcut menu appears below the Ask a Question box, as shown in Figure 10.1.

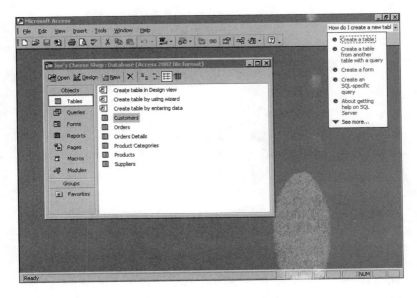

**FIGURE 10.1**
*The Ask a Question box provides a list of Help topics that you can quickly access.*

To access one of the Help topics supplied on the shortcut menu, click that particular topic. The Help window opens with topical matches for that keyword or phrase displayed.

In the case of the "new table" question used in Figure 10.1 you could select **Create a table** from the shortcut menu that appears. This opens the Help window and displays help on how to create a new Access table (see Figure 10.2).

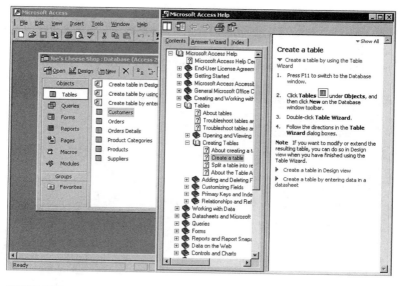

**FIGURE 10.2**
*The Ask a Question box provides a quick way to access the Help window.*

In the Help window, you can use the links provided to navigate the Help system. Click any of the content links to expand the information provided on that particular topic. You can also use the Contents, Answer Wizard, and Index tabs to find additional information or look for new information in the Help window. You learn more about these different Help window tabs later in this lesson.

## USING THE OFFICE ASSISTANT

Another way to get help in Access is to use the Office Assistant. The Office Assistant supplies the same type of access to the Help system as the Ask a Question box. You ask the Office Assistant a question, and it supplies you with a list of possible answers that provide links to various Help topics. The next two sections discuss how to use the Office Assistant.

## TURNING THE OFFICE ASSISTANT ON AND OFF

By default, the Office Assistant is off. To show the Office Assistant in your application window, select the **Help** menu and then select **Show the Office Assistant**.

You can also quickly hide the Office Assistant if you no longer want it in your application window. Right-click the Office Assistant and select **Hide**. If you want to get rid of the Office Assistant completely so it isn't activated when you select the Help feature, right-click the Office Assistant and select **Options**. Clear the **Use the Office Assistant** check box, and then click **OK**. You can always get the Office Assistant back by selecting **Help**, **Show Office Assistant**.

## ASKING THE OFFICE ASSISTANT A QUESTION

When you click the Office Assistant, a balloon appears above it. Type a question into the text box. For example, you might type **How do I print?** for help printing your work. Click the **Search** button.

The Office Assistant provides some topics that reference Help topics in the Help system. Click the option that best describes what you're trying to do. The Help window appears, containing more detailed information. Use the Help window to get the exact information that you need.

Although not everyone likes the Office Assistant because having it enabled means that it is always sitting in your Access application window, it can be useful at times. For example, when you access particular features in Access, the Office Assistant can automatically provide you with context-sensitive help on that particular feature. If you are brand-new to Microsoft Access, you might want to use the Office Assistant to help you learn the various features that Access provides as you use them.

**Select Your Own Office Assistant**    Several different Office Assistants are available in Microsoft Office. To select your favorite, click the Office Assistant and select the **Options** button. On the Office Assistant dialog box that appears, select the **Gallery** tab. Click the **Next** button repeatedly to see the different Office Assistants that are available. When you locate the assistant you want to use, click **OK**.

## USING THE HELP WINDOW

You can also forgo either the Type a Question box or the Office Assistant and get your help directly from the Help window. To directly access the Help window, select **Help** and then **Microsoft Access Help**. You can also press the **F1** key to make the Help window appear.

The Help window provides two panes. The pane on the left provides three tabs: Contents, Answer Wizard, and Index. The right pane of the Help window provides either help subject matter or links to different Help topics. It functions a great deal like a Web browser window. You click a link to a particular body of information and that information appears in the right pane.

The first thing that you should do is maximize the Help window by clicking its **Maximize** button. This makes it easier to locate and read the information that the Help system provides (see Figure 10.3).

When you first open the Help window, a group of links in the right pane provides you with access to information about new Access features and other links, such as a link to Microsoft's Office Web site. Next, take a look at how you can take advantage of different ways to find information in the Help window: the Contents tab, the Answer Wizard tab, and the Index tab.

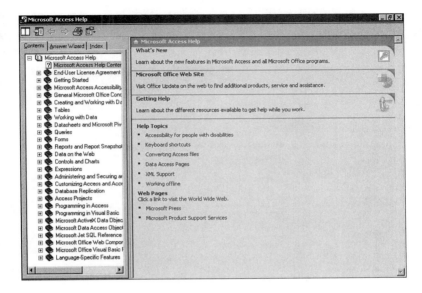

**FIGURE 10.3**
*The Help window provides access to all the help information provided for Access.*

TIP

> **View the Help Window Tabs**    If you don't see the differ-
> ent tabs in the Help window, click the **Show** button on
> the Help window toolbar.

## USING THE CONTENTS TAB

The Contents tab of the Help system is a series of books you can
open. Each book has one or more Help topics in it, which appear as
pages or chapters. To select a Help topic from the Contents tab, follow
these steps:

1. In the Help window, click the **Contents** tab on the left side of
   the Help window.

2. Find the book that describes, in broad terms, the subject for
   which you need help.

**3.** Double-click the book, and a list of Help topics appears below the book, as shown in Figure 10.4.

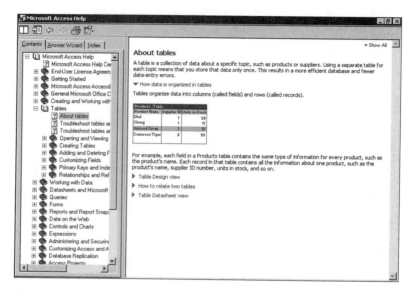

**FIGURE 10.4**
*Use the Contents tab to browse through the various Help topics.*

**4.** Click one of the pages (the pages contain a question mark) under a Help topic to display it in the right pane of the Help window.

**5.** When you finish reading a topic, select another topic on the Contents tab or click the Help window's **Close (x)** button to exit Help.

## Using the Answer Wizard

Another way to get help in the Help window is to use the Answer Wizard. The Answer Wizard works the same as the Ask a Question box or the Office Assistant; you ask the wizard questions and it supplies you with a list of topics that relate to your question. You click one of the choices provided to view help in the Help window.

To get help using the Answer Wizard, follow these steps:

1. Click the **Answer Wizard** tab in the Help window.

2. Type your question into the What Would You Like to Do? box. For example, you might type the question, **How do I filter a table?**

3. After typing your question, click the **Search** button. A list of topics appears in the Select Topic to Display box. Select a particular topic, and its information appears in the right pane of the Help window, as shown in Figure 10.5.

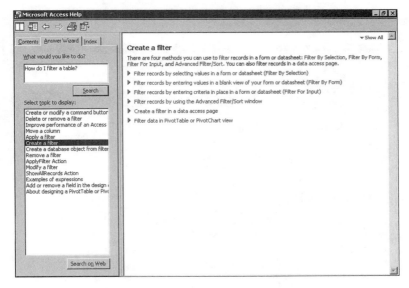

**FIGURE 10.5**
*Search for help in the Help window using the Answer Wizard tab.*

**TIP**

> **Print Help**    If you want to print information provided in the Help window, click the **Print** icon on the Help toolbar.

## USING THE INDEX

The Index is an alphabetical listing of every Help topic available. It's like an index in a book.

Follow these steps to use the index:

1. In the Help window, click the **Index** tab.

2. Type the first few letters of the topic for which you are look-ing. The Or Choose Keywords box jumps quickly to a key-word that contains the characters you have typed.

3. Double-click the appropriate keyword in the keywords box. Topics for that keyword appear in the Choose a Topic box.

4. Click a topic to view help in the right pane of the Help window (see Figure 10.6).

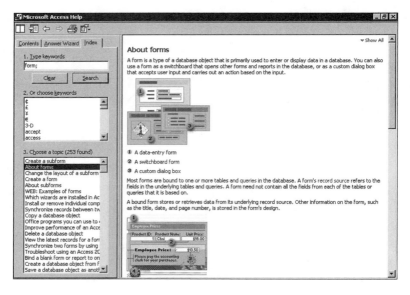

**FIGURE 10.6**
*Use the Index tab to get help in the Help window.*

**TIP**

Navigation Help Topics     You can move from topic to
topic in the right pane of the Help window by clicking
the various links that are provided there. Some topics
are collapsed. Click the triangle next to the topic to
expand the topic and view the help provided.

## GETTING HELP WITH SCREEN ELEMENTS

If you wonder about the function of a particular button or tool on the
Access screen, wonder no more. Just follow these steps to learn about
this part of Help:

1. Select **Help** and then **What's This?** or press **Shift+F1**. The
   mouse pointer changes to an arrow with a question mark.

2. Click the screen element for which you want help. A box
   appears explaining the element.

**TIP**

Take Advantage of ScreenTips     Another Help feature provided by Access is the ScreenTip. All the buttons on the
different toolbars provided by Access have a ScreenTip.
Place the mouse on a particular button or icon, and the
name of the item (which often helps you determine its
function) appears in a ScreenTip.

In this lesson you learned how to use the Access Help feature. In the
next lesson you learn how to create relationships between database
tables.

# LESSON 11
# Creating Relationships Between Tables

*In this lesson, you learn how to link two or more tables using a common field and create a relational database.*

## UNDERSTANDING TABLE RELATIONSHIPS

You've already learned in Lesson 2, "Working in Access," that the best way to design a database is to create tables that hold discrete types of information. For example, one table can contain customer information, and another table can hold order information. By creating relationships between tables, you enable forms, queries, and reports to combine information from the tables to produce meaningful results.

Suppose that you have two tables in your database. One table, Customers, contains names and addresses; the other, Orders, contains orders the customers have placed. The two tables both contain a common field: Customer ID. All records in the Orders table correspond to a record in the Customers table. (This is called a one-to-many relationship because one customer could have many orders.)

The secret to creating relationships revolves around the primary keys for your tables. For example, in a Customers table, the primary key is the Customer ID. It uniquely identifies each customer record. Then, when you design an Orders table, you make sure that you include the Customer ID field. In the Orders table, the Customer ID is not the primary key (it is actually called the foreign key); a field such as Order Number would be the primary key field. You include the Customer ID field in the Orders table so that order information can be linked to customer information in the Customers table.

**PLAIN ENGLISH**

> **Foreign Key**   A primary key field in a table that is duplicated in a second table (where it is not the primary key) and used to link the tables together.

## CREATING A RELATIONSHIP BETWEEN TABLES

To create a relationship between tables, open the Relationships window. Before you can create relationships between tables, you must first add the tables to the Relationships window. Follow these steps:

1. In the database, select **Tools, Relationships**, or click the **Relationships** button on the toolbar to open the Relationships window.

2. If you haven't selected any tables yet, the Show Table dialog box appears automatically (see Figure 11.1). If it doesn't appear, choose **Relationships, Show Table**.

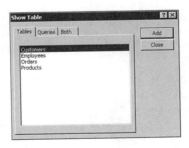

**FIGURE 11.1**
*Add tables to your Relationships window with the Show Table dialog box.*

3. Click a table that you want to include in the Relationships window, and then click the **Add** button.

**TIP**

> **Well-Designed Databases and Relationships**   In a well-designed database, every table in the database is related to at least one other table in the database. So, you might want to add all your tables to the Relationships window.

4. Repeat step 3 to select all the tables you require in the Relationships window, and then click **Close**. Each table appears in its own box in the Relationships window, as shown in Figure 11.2. Each table box lists all the fields in that table.

**TIP**

> **Enlarge the Table Box**   If you can't see all the fields in a table's box, drag the table border to make it large enough to see all the fields.

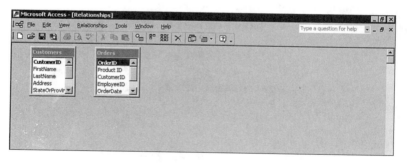

**FIGURE 11.2**
*Tables in the Relationships window.*

5. After you have the tables available in the relationships window, you can create the relationships between the table. Remember that you must link the tables using a common field. For example, you can link the Customers table to the

Orders table using the Customer ID field, as shown in Figure 11.2. Select the common field in the table where it is the primary key (in this case, the Customer table). Drag the field and drop it on its counterpart (the same field name) in the other table (in this case Orders). The Edit Relationships window opens (see Figure 11.3).

**CAUTION**

**Field Type Matters**    The fields to be linked must be of the same data type (date, number, text, and so on). The only exception is that you can link a field with an AutoNumber format to another field with a number format; AutoNumber fields are considered long-integer number fields.

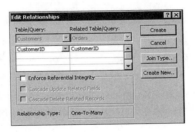

**FIGURE 11.3**
*The Edit Relationships dialog box asks you to define the relationship you're creating.*

6. The Edit Relationships dialog box shows the fields that will be related. It also allows you to enforce referential integrity, which you learn about in the next section. For now, click **Create**. A relationship is created, and you'll see a join line between the two fields in the Relationships window (see Figure 11.4).

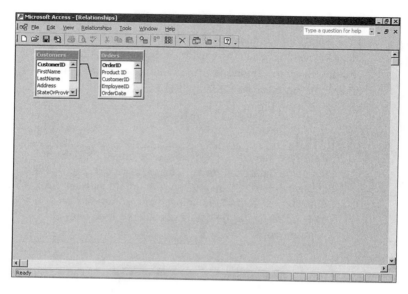

**FIGURE 11.4**
*The join line represents a relationship between the two fields.*

 When you create relationships between tables, it's important that you save them. Click the **Save** button on the Relationships toolbar to save the current relationships (and the list of tables available in the Relationships window).

## ENFORCING REFERENTIAL INTEGRITY

In the Edit Relationships box is a check box called Enforce Referential Integrity. What does this mean? *Referential integrity* means that data entered in a field that is used to link two tables must match from one table to another. Actually, the data entered in the table where the field does not serve as the primary key must match the entries that are in the table where the field serves as the primary key.

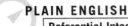

**PLAIN ENGLISH**

> **Referential Integrity**    The data contained in a primary
> key field used in a table relationship must be matched
> in that same field in the secondary table. Otherwise,
> Access returns an error message.

For example, you could link a Customers table that has a Customer ID field as its primary key to an Orders table that also holds the Customer ID field, where it does not serve as the primary key (the Customer ID is providing the link for the relationship). If you enforce referential integrity, values entered into the Order table's Customer ID field must match values already entered into the Customers table's Customer ID field. Enforcing referential integrity is a way to make sure that data is entered correctly into the secondary table.

When referential integrity is breached during data entry, (meaning a value is entered into the secondary table in the relationship that was not in the linking field of the primary table), an error message appears (see Figure 11.5). This error message lets you know that the field value you have entered in the linking field is not contained in a record in the other table in the relationship (where the field is the primary key).

**FIGURE 11.5**
*Enforcing referential integrity means that values entered in the linking field must be contained in the field in the table where it serves as the primary key.*

Two other options are possible when data entered into a field violates referential integrity. Figure 11.6 shows the Edit Relationships with the Enforce Referential Integrity box selected. The two additional options provided are

- **Cascade Update Related Fields**—If this check box is selected, any data changes that you make to the linking field in the primary table (Customers, in this example) are updated to the secondary table. For example, if you had a customer in the Customers table listed with Customer ID 5 and you changed that to Customer ID 6, any references to Customer ID 5 would be updated to Customer ID 6 in the Orders table.

- **Cascade Delete Related Fields**—If this check box is marked and you change the linking field's data in the primary table so that it no longer matches in the secondary table, the field information is deleted from the secondary table. Therefore, if you changed a Customer ID number in the Customers table, the field data in the Customer ID field in the Orders table would be deleted.

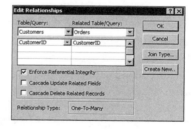

**FIGURE 11.6**
*The Edit Relationships dialog box is used to change the options related to a particular relationship.*

You should probably set up your relationships and enforce referential integrity before you do any data entry in the related tables. You should also typically enter the data first into the table where the linking field is the primary key. For example, you should fill in as much of your Customers table information as possible before you try to fill the data fields in the related Orders table.

## Editing a Relationship

You can edit any of the relationships that you create between your tables. Just double-click the relationship line and the Edit Relationships dialog box appears (refer to Figure 9.6). For example, you might want to enforce referential integrity on an existing relationship or change other options related to the relationship as discussed in the previous section.

When you have finished editing the relationship, click **OK** to close the Edit Relationships box. This returns you to the Relationships window.

## Removing a Relationship

To delete a relationship, just click it in the Relationships window (the line between the tables turns bold to indicate that it is selected), and then press **Delete**. Access asks for confirmation; click **Yes**, and the relationship disappears.

If you delete relationships between tables, you are affecting how information in the tables can be combined in a query, form, or report. It is a good practice to design your tables so that they can be related. Remember that each table is supposed to hold a subset of the database information. If each table is set up correctly, it should have at least one other table in the database to which it can be related.

In this lesson, you learned how to create, edit, and delete relationships between tables. In the next lesson, you learn how to create forms using a wizard or from scratch.

# LESSON 12
# Creating a Simple Form

*In this lesson, you learn how to create a form using the AutoForm, the Form Wizard, and from scratch.*

## CREATING FORMS

As discussed in Lesson 7, "Entering Data into a Table," entering data directly into a table has its downside. It can become difficult to concentrate on one record at a time, and if you are working with a large number of fields, information is constantly scrolling on and off the screen.

An alternative to entering data into the table is to use a form. With a form, you can allot as much space as you need for each field, you get to concentrate on one record at a time, and you can create forms that simultaneously enter data into more than one table. You can create a form in three ways:

- AutoForms provide very quick, generic forms that contain all the fields in a single table.

- The Form Wizard helps you create a form by providing a series of screens in which you can choose the fields and style for the form.

- Creating a form from scratch means that you work in the Form Design view and select the fields from the appropriate table or tables. This is the most difficult way to create a new form (at first), but it also provides the most control.

# CREATING A FORM WITH AUTOFORM

The easiest way to create a form is with AutoForm. AutoForm takes the fields from a specified table and creates a form; it's not very flexible, but it is very convenient. To use the AutoForm feature, follow these steps:

1. From the database window, click the **Forms** object type.

2. Click the **New** button on the database window toolbar. The New Form dialog box appears (see Figure 12.1).

**FIGURE 12.1**
*Choose how you want to create your form.*

3. You can click several types of forms, including

   - **AutoForm:Columnar**—A columnar form (the most popular kind). This creates a form that contains your fields in a single column, from top to bottom.

   - **AutoForm:Tabular**—A form that resembles a table.

   - **AutoForm:Datasheet**—A form that resembles a datasheet.

4. Open the drop-down list at the bottom of the dialog box and choose the table or query you want to use as the source of the form's fields.

5. Click **OK**. The form appears, ready for data entry (see Figure 12.2).

**FIGURE 12.2**
*AutoForm creates a form based on a single table.*

Forms created with AutoForm can be edited using the Form Design view, which is discussed later in this lesson. When you attempt to close the AutoForm, you are asked whether you want to save it. If you do, click **Yes**. Then, enter a name for the form into the Save As box and click **OK**.

**TIP**

 **Create an AutoForm in the Table Datasheet View** You can also create an AutoForm while you are working on a table in the Datasheet view. Click the **AutoForm** button on the Table Datasheet toolbar. A new form appears, based on the table's fields.

## CREATING A FORM WITH THE FORM WIZARD

The Form Wizard offers a good compromise between the automation of AutoForm and the control of creating a form from scratch. The wizard allows you to select the fields for the form and select the layout and look for the form. Follow these steps to use the Form Wizard:

1. From the database window, click the **Forms** object type.

2. Double-click **Create Form by Using Wizard** to open the Form Wizard (see Figure 12.3).

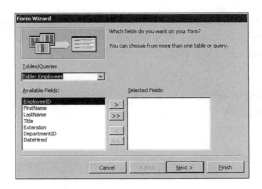

**FIGURE 12.3**
*The Form Wizard enables you to choose which fields you want to include from as many different tables in the database as you like.*

3. From the Tables/Queries drop-down list, choose a table or query from which to select fields. (By default, the first table in alphabetical order is selected, which probably isn't what you want.)

4. Click a field in the Available Fields list that you want to include on the form, and then click the **Add** (>) button to move it to the Selected Fields list.

5. Repeat step 4 until you've selected all the fields you want to include from that table. If you want to include fields from another table or query, go back to step 3 and choose another table.

**PLAIN ENGLISH**

**Selecting All Fields**   You can quickly move all the fields from the Available Fields list to the Selected Fields list by clicking the **Add All** (>>) button. If you make a mistake, you can remove a field from the Selected Fields list by clicking it and then clicking either the **Remove** (<) button or the **Remove All** (<<) button.

6. Click **Next** to continue. You're asked to choose a layout: **Columnar**, **Tabular**, **Datasheet**, or **Justified**. Click each button to see a preview of that type (Columnar is the most common). Select the layout you want to use, and then click **Next**.

7. The next screen asks you to select a style for your form (see Figure 12.4). Click each style listed to see a preview of it; click **Next** when you've selected a style.

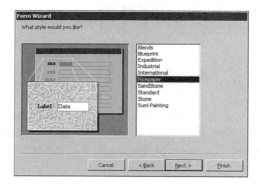

**FIGURE 12.4**
*You can select from several form styles.*

8. On the last screen, enter a title for the form into the text box at the top of the dialog box (if you want a title other than the default).

9. Click the **Finish** button. The form appears, ready for data entry (see Figure 12.5).

**FIGURE 12.5**
*The Form Wizard creates a usable form using the fields, format, and style that you selected.*

If your form's field labels are cut off or need some additional layout work, you can fix them in the Form Design view. You learn about modifying a form in Lesson 13, "Modifying a Form."

## CREATING A FORM FROM SCRATCH

You can also create a form from scratch in the Form Design view. This method might seem difficult at first, but Access provides tools, such as the Field list and the Toolbox, to help you create your form. The most powerful and difficult way to create a form is with Form Design view. In this view, you decide exactly where to place each field and how to format it.

To open the Form Design view and create a new form, follow these steps:

1. From the database window, click the **Forms** object type.

2. Click the **New** button. The New Form dialog box appears.

3. Click **Design View**.

4. Select a table or query from the drop-down list at the bottom of the dialog box. This table provides a Field list that makes it easy to place fields on the form.

5. Click **OK**. A Form Design window appears (see Figure 12.6). You're ready to create your form.

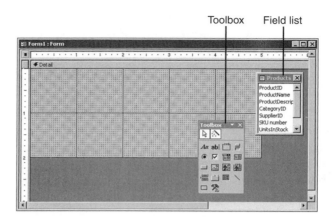

**FIGURE 12.6**

*Form Design view presents a blank canvas for your new form.*

Notice that a Field list and Toolbox appear in the Form Design view. You work with creating form controls (the equivalent of a field in a table) using these tools in the next section.

You can also start the process of building a form in the Design view by double-clicking the **Create Form in Design View** link in the database window. Because you are not specifying a table for the Field list to use (as you did in the steps outlined in this section), however, that Field list won't be available. Instead, you must specify a table for the Field list.

 To do this, click the **Properties** button on the Form Design toolbar. The form's properties dialog box appears (see Figure 12.7).

**FIGURE 12.7**
*The properties dialog box enables you to set a number of properties for the form.*

In the properties dialog box, be sure that the **All** tab is selected. Click in the Record Source box, and then use the drop-down arrow that appears to specify the table that will serve as the field source for the form. The Field list appears. Close the properties dialog box.

**TIP**

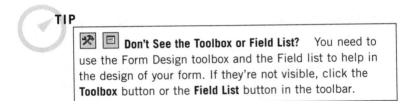

**Don't See the Toolbox or Field List?**   You need to use the Form Design toolbox and the Field list to help in the design of your form. If they're not visible, click the **Toolbox** button or the **Field List** button in the toolbar.

## Adding Controls to a Form

The basic idea of the Form Design window is simple: It's similar to a light table or a paste-up board where you place the elements of your form. The fields you add to a form appear in the form's Detail area. The Detail area is the only area visible at first; you'll learn how to add other areas in the next lesson.

### PLAIN ENGLISH

**Controls and Fields**    When you are working with a table, you work directly with fields of data. On forms and reports, you work with controls, which are elements that display data from a field, hold informative text (such as titles and labels), or are purely decorative (such as lines and rectangles).

To add a control displaying a field to the form, follow these steps:

1. Display the Field list if it's not showing. Choose the **Field List** from the **View** menu to do so.

2. Drag a field from the Field list onto the Detail area of the form. The mouse pointer changes to show that a field is being placed.

3. Repeat step 2 to add as many fields as you like to the form (see Figure 12.8).

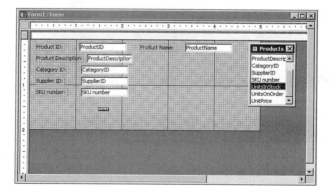

**FIGURE 12.8**
*Drag fields from the Field list to the form grid.*

When you drag a field to a form from the Field list, it becomes a control that displays data from that table field on the form. It is basically a link between the table field and the control on the form. You can drag more than one field to the form at once using the steps described earlier. However, in step 2, rather than clicking and dragging a single field, do one of the following before dragging:

- To select a block of adjacent fields, click the first one you want and hold down the **Shift** key while you click the last one.

- To select nonadjacent fields, hold down the **Ctrl** key as you click each one you want.

- To select all the fields on the list, double-click the **Field List** title bar.

You can move objects around on a form after you initially place them; you'll learn how to do this in the next lesson. Don't worry if your form doesn't look very professional at this point; in the next several lessons, you see how to modify and improve your form.

**TIP**

**Using Snap to Grid**    If you find it hard to align the fields neatly, choose **Snap to Grid** from the **Format** menu to place a check mark next to that command. This forces the borders of the fields included on your form to "snap" to the grid that appears in the Design view. If you want to align the fields on your own, select **Snap to Grid** again to turn it off.

After you have placed all the controls on the form that relate to the fields in a particular table or tables, you are ready to do some data entry. First, however, you must save the form's structure. Click the **Save** button on the Form Design toolbar. Type a name for the form into the Save As dialog box. Then click **OK**.

## ENTERING DATA INTO A FORM

The point of creating a form is so that you can enter data more easily into your tables. The form acts as an attractive mask that shields you from the stark reality of the table's Datasheet view. To enter data into a form, follow these steps:

1. Open the form. In the database window, click the **Form** tab, and then double-click the form's name.

2. Click in the field with which you want to begin and type your data.

3. Press **Tab** to move to the next field. If you need to go back, you can press **Shift+Tab** to move to the previous field. When you reach the last field, pressing **Tab** moves you to the first field in a new, blank record.

   To move to the next record before you reach the bottom field or to move back to previous records, click the right- and left-arrow buttons on the left end of the navigation bar at the bottom of the window.

4. Repeat steps 2 and 3 to enter all the records you like. They're saved automatically as you enter them.

In this lesson, you created a form using AutoForm, the Form Wizard and from scratch in the Design view. In the next lesson, you learn how to modify and fine-tune your forms.

# LESSON 13
# Modifying a Form

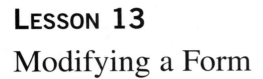

*In this lesson, you learn how to modify a form's design.*

## CLEANING UP YOUR FORM: AN OVERVIEW

After you've created a form, you might find that it doesn't quite look as good as you like. Controls might need realignment, or you might want to resize the label for a particular control or controls. You also might want to expand the form grid areas so that you can rearrange the form controls or add additional controls to the form.

All these actions can be accomplished in the Form Design view. Using this view, you can edit the structure of any form that you create, regardless of whether you created the form using AutoForm, the Form Wizard, or the Design view.

## MOVING FIELD CONTROLS

The most common change to a form is to reposition a control. For example, you might want to move several controls down so you can insert a new control, or you might want to rearrange how the controls appear on the grid.

If you placed controls on the form to begin with (rather than using AutoForm or the Form Wizard), you have probably noticed that the control consists of two parts: a label and the actual control. You can manipulate various aspects of the label and the control independently (such as their sizes or the distance between them). You work with label and control sizing later in this lesson.

**TIP**

> **More Space**    If you want to create extra space at the
> bottom of the controls so that you have more room to
> move them around, drag the Form Footer pane down so
> that more of the Detail area is visible. You can also drag
> the right side of the grid to make the form wider. If you
> need more space at the top of the form, highlight all the
> controls and move them down as a group.

Follow these steps:

1. From the database window, select a form in the Form list,
   and then click the **Design** button on the database window
   toolbar. The form is opened in Design view.

2. Click a control's label to select it. Selection handles appear
   around the label (a displacement handle also appears on the
   control, but you don't want to touch that right now). You can
   select several controls by holding down **Shift** as you click
   each control's label.

3. Position the mouse pointer on the edge of the control's label
   so that the pointer becomes a hand (see Figure 13.1). If
   you're moving more than one selected control, you can position the mouse pointer on any selected control's label.

4. Drag the control's label and the control to a new location.

5. Release the mouse button when the control is at the desired
   new location.

**CAUTION**

> **The Label Moved Without the Control Attached!**    When
> you position the mouse pointer over the control to be
> moved, be sure the pointer changes to an open hand, as
> shown in Figure 13.1. If you see a pointing finger, you
> are on the control's displacement box. The pointing fin-
> ger is used to move controls and labels independently,
> as you'll learn in the next section.

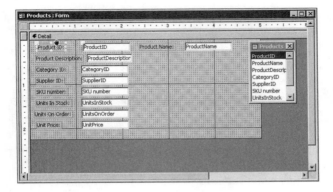

**FIGURE 13.1**
*To move a control, first select it. Then, drag it by its label using the hand pointer.*

## Moving Controls and Field Labels Independently

Depending on how you are laying out the controls in your form, you might want to separate the control label from the control. For example, you might want to arrange the form in a tabular format where the control names are positioned over the controls. Separating controls and labels also allows you to move the control so that the field label isn't cut off. Then you can resize the label.

### PLAIN ENGLISH

**Field Controls: The Most Commonly Used Controls**   Controls related to fields in a table and their attached labels are discussed in this lesson, but the same methods can be used with other controls that have attached labels, such as combo boxes and list boxes (which are discussed in Lesson 14, "Adding Special Controls to Forms").

To move a control or its attached label by itself, follow these steps:

1. Click the control that you want to separate from its label.

2. Position the mouse pointer over the displacement handle at the top left of the label or the control (the large box handle on the top left of the label or the control). The mouse pointer becomes a pointing finger (see Figure 13.2).

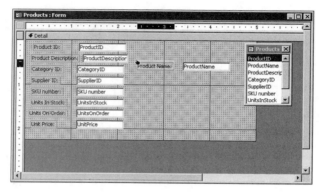

**FIGURE 13.2**
*Drag the displacement handle to move the control or label independently.*

3. Drag the label or the control to a new position.

**TIP**

**Deleting Labels**    If a certain control is self-explanatory (such as a picture), you might want to delete its attached label. To do so, select the label and press **Delete**.

Separating the label from a control allows you to arrange your controls in all kinds of tabular and columnar arrangements on the form grid. Just make sure that you keep the correct label in close proximity to the appropriate control.

## CHANGING LABEL AND CONTROL SIZES

You can also change the width or height of a label or control. Separating a label from its control, as discussed in the previous section, provides you with the room to resize the label or the control independently. To change a label's or control's width (length), follow these steps:

1. Click the label or the control to select it. If you are going to resize the control itself, be sure you click the control. Selection handles (small boxes) appear around it.

2. Position the mouse pointer on either the right or left of the label or control until the mouse pointer becomes a sizing tool (a horizontal double-headed arrow, as shown in Figure 13.3).

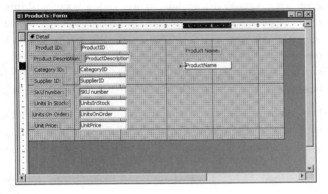

**FIGURE 13.3**
*You can change the size of a label or control by dragging a sizing box.*

3. Drag the label's or control's sizing handle to increase or decrease the length as needed. Then release the mouse button.

## VIEWING HEADERS AND FOOTERS

So far, you have been working in the main part of the form grid called the Detail area. The Detail area is where you place the various field controls for the form (and additional controls, such as those discussed in the next lesson).

There are other areas of a form. For example, a form header can be used to include a title for the form (header information appears at the top of the form). The other form areas are

- **Form Header**—An area at the top of the form that can be used for repeating information, such as a form title.

- **Form Footer**—An area at the bottom of the form that can be used for repeating information, such as the current date or explanatory information related to the form.

- **Page Header**—Forms that are built to add data to multiple tables can consist of multiple pages. You can also include a Page Header area on a form that enables you to include information that you want to repeat on each page of the form when it is printed out, such as your name or company information.

- **Page Footer**—This area enables you to place information, such as page numbering, that appears on every page when the form is printed.

These different areas of the form grid aren't displayed by default; to display these areas, such as the Form Header/Footer, use the View menu. To show the Form Header/Footer, for example, select **View**, **Form Header/Footer**.

When you create a form with the Form Wizard, the Form Header and Form Footer areas appear in Design view, but nothing is in them. To make some room to work in the Form Header, click the **Detail Header** bar to select it, position the mouse pointer between the bars, and drag downward (see Figure 13.4).

The Detail section contains controls whose data changes with every record. As already mentioned, the Form Header contains text you want repeated on each onscreen form. This makes the Form Header a great place to add a label that contains a title for the form.

Sizing tool                              Form Header

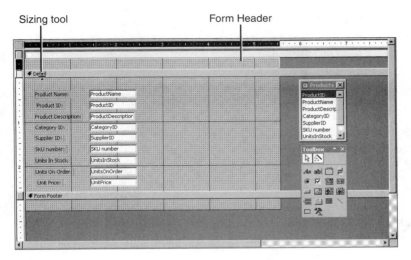

**FIGURE 13.4**
*Drag the Detail Header bar down to create space to add text in the Form header.*

## ADDING LABELS

You can add a label to any of the areas in the form. Adding labels to the form enables you to place titles, subtitles, or explanatory text on the form. Because you will want these types of labels to repeat at the top or bottom of the form, the best place to add them is to the form's header or footer. To add titles and other general information to a header or a footer or to add information specific to particular controls to the Detail area, follow these steps:

1. If the toolbox isn't displayed, choose **Toolbox** from the **View** menu, or click the **Toolbox** button on the toolbar.

2. Click the **Label** tool in the toolbox (the one with the italicized letters *Aa* on it). The mouse pointer changes to a capital A with a plus sign next to it.

3. Place the Label pointer on an area of the form grid, such as the Form Header area. Drag to create a box or rectangle for text entry (see Figure 13.5).

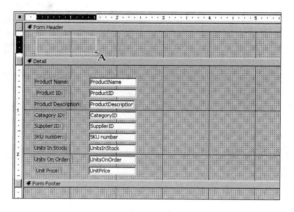

**FIGURE 13.5**
*Select the Label tool in the toolbox.*

4. When you release the mouse button, a new label box appears with an insertion point inside it. Type the text you want the label box to contain.

### PLAIN ENGLISH

**You Must Type the Text Now**    If you don't type anything before you go on to step 5, the box disappears as soon as you click away from it.

5. Click anywhere outside the control's area to finish, or press **Enter**.

Don't worry about positioning the label as you create it; you can move a label control in the same way that you move other controls. Just click it, position the mouse pointer so that the hand appears, and then drag it to where you want it to go.

## FORMATTING TEXT ON A FORM

After you place all your information on the form (that is, the controls you want to include and labels to display any titles or explanatory text), the next step is to make the form look more appealing.

All the formatting tools you need are on the Formatting toolbar (the top toolbar in the Form Design view). Table 13.1 describes several of the formatting tools. To format a control or label, select it, and then click the appropriate formatting tool to apply the format to the control or label.

**TABLE 13.1**   Tools on the Formatting Toolbar

| Tool | Purpose |
|------|---------|
| **B** | Toggles bold on/off |
| *I* | Toggles italic on/off |
| U | Toggles underline on/off |
| ≣ | Left-aligns text |
| ≣ | Centers text |
| ≣ | Right-aligns text |
| ◇ | Fills the selected box with the selected color |
| A | Colors the text in the selected box |
| ✎ | Colors the outline of the selected box |
| ▢ | Adds a border to the selected box |
| ▭ | Adds a special effect to the selected box |

Some tools, such as the Font and Size tools, are drop-down lists. You click the down arrow next to the tool and then select from the list. Other tools are simple buttons for turning bold and italic on or off. Still other tools, such as the Color and Border tools, combine a button and a drop-down list. If you click the button, it applies the current value. You can click the down arrow next to the button to change the value.

You can change the color of the form background, too. Just click the header for the section you want to change (for example, **Detail**) to select the entire section. Then right-click and choose **Fill/Back** color to change the color.

### PLAIN ENGLISH

**AutoFormat**    You can use a shortcut for formatting your form. Choose **Format, AutoFormat**. You can choose from among several premade color and formatting schemes. If you don't like the formatting after you apply it, press **Ctrl+Z** to undo.

## Changing Tab Order

When you enter data on a form, press **Tab** to move from control to control in the order they're shown in the form. The progression from control to control on the form is the *tab order*. When you first create a form, the tab order runs from top to bottom.

When you move and rearrange controls, the tab order doesn't change automatically. For example, suppose you had 10 controls arranged in a column and you rearranged them so that the tenth one was at the beginning. It would still require 10 presses of the **Tab** key to move the insertion point to that control, even though it's now at the top of the form. This makes it more difficult to fill in the form, so you'll want to adjust the tab order to reflect the new structure of the form.

**TIP**

> **Tab Order Improvements**   To make data entry easier, you might want to change the tab order to be different from the obvious top-to-bottom structure. For example, if 90% of the records you enter skip several controls, you might want to put those controls last in the tab order so that you can skip over them easily.

Follow these steps to adjust the tab order:

1. Choose **View**, **Tab Order**. The Tab Order dialog box appears (see Figure 13.6).

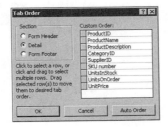

**FIGURE 13.6**
*Use the Tab Order dialog box to decide what tab order to use on your form.*

2. Choose the section for which you want to set tab order. The default is Detail.

3. The controls appear in their tab order. To change the order, click a control and then drag it up or down in the list.

4. To quickly set the tab order based on the controls' current positions in the form (top to bottom), click the **Auto Order** button.

5. Click **OK**.

When you have finished making different enhancements to your form, you must save the changes. Click the **Save** button on the Form Design toolbar.

In this lesson, you learned how to improve a form by moving controls, adding text labels, adding formatting, and adjusting the tab order. In the next lesson, you learn about special controls that you can add to a form.

# LESSON 14

# Adding Special Controls to Forms

*In this lesson, you learn about some special controls you can include on your forms.*

## USING SPECIAL FORM CONTROLS

So far, you've taken a look at adding controls to a form that directly relate to fields on a table or tables. This means that unless the control is linked to a field in a table that uses the AutoNumber data type, you are going to have to type absolutely all the data that you enter into the form (exactly as you would in the table).

Fortunately, Access offers some special form controls that can be used to help you enter data. For example, a list box can contain a list of entries for a control. All you have to do is select the appropriate entry from the list. Other special controls also exist that can make it easier to get your data into the form. These controls are

- **List Box**—Presents a list from which you choose an item.

- **Combo Group**—Like a list box, but you can type in other entries in addition to those on the list.

- **Option Group**—Provides you with different types of input buttons (you can select only one type of button when you create an Option group). You can use option buttons, toggle buttons, or check boxes.

- **Command Button**—Performs some function when you click it, such as starting another program, printing a report, saving the record, or anything else you specify.

Figure 14.1 shows some special controls in the Form view. In this lesson, you create each of these control types.

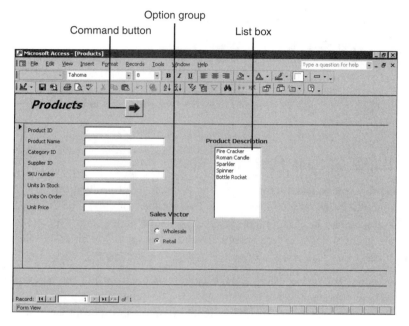

**FIGURE 14.1**
*Special controls can make data entry easier.*

All these special controls can be created using the buttons on the Toolbox. Wizards are also available that walk you through the steps of creating each of these special control types. To use the wizard for a particular special control, make sure that the Control Wizards button is activated on the Toolbox. Figure 14.2 shows the Toolbox and the buttons that you are working with in this lesson.

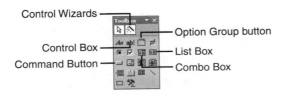

Control Wizards
Control Box
Command Button

Option Group button
List Box
Combo Box

**FIGURE 14.2**
*To use wizards, make sure that the Control Wizards button is selected.*

## CREATING A LIST BOX OR A COMBO BOX

A *list box* or a *combo box* can come in handy if you find yourself repeatedly typing certain values into a field. For example, if you have to enter the name of one of your 12 branch offices each time you use a form, you might find it easier to create a list box containing the branch office names, and then you can click to select a particular name from the list. With a list box, the person doing the data entry is limited to the choices that display on the list.

A combo box is useful when a list box is appropriate, but when it's possible that a different entry might occasionally be needed. For example, if most of your customers come from one of six states, but occasionally you get a new customer from another state, you might use a combo box. During data entry, you could choose the state from the list when appropriate and type a new state when it's not.

Follow these steps to create a list box or combo box from Form Design view:

1. Make sure that the **Control Wizards** button on the Toolbox is selected.

2. Click the **List Box** or **Combo Box** button in the Toolbox. The mouse pointer changes to show the type of box you selected.

3. Drag your mouse to draw a box on the grid where you want the new element to be placed. When you release the mouse button, the list or combo box wizard starts.

4. On the wizard's first screen (see Figure 14.3), click the
   option button **I Will Type In the Values That I Want**. Then
   click **Next**.

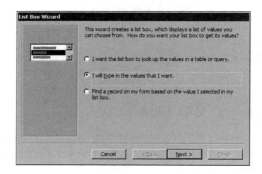

**FIGURE 14.3**
*The wizard walks you through the steps of creating a list box or a combo box.*

**TIP**

> **Another Way to Enter Values**    List boxes and combo
> boxes can also be set up so that they pull their list of
> values from an existing table in the database (or a query
> that you've created). Select **I Want the List Box to Look Up
> the Values in a Table or Query** on the first wizard screen,
> and then specify the table or query that should supply
> the values for the list.

5. On the next screen, a column of boxes (only one box shows
   before you enter your values) is provided that you use to
   enter the values that you want to appear in the list. Type them
   in (as shown in Figure 14.4), pressing the **Tab** key after each
   one. Then click **Next**.

6. On the next screen, you choose the option of Access either
   remembering the values in the list for later use (such as in a
   calculation) or entering a value selected from the list in a

particular field. Because you are using this box for data entry, select **Store That Value in This Field**, and then choose a field from the drop-down list that is supplied. For example, if you want this list to provide data from your Product Description field, select it in the drop-down list. Click **Next** to continue.

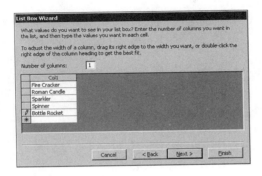

**FIGURE 14.4**
*Type the values for the list or combo box.*

**TIP**

> **Tying a List or Combo Box to a Field**    The best way to approach list and combo boxes is to create a form that includes all the fields from a particular table. Then, you can delete the controls for fields in the Form Design view that you want to "re-create" as list or combo boxes. You then store the values from the list or combo box in one of the fields that you removed from the form.

7. On the next screen, type the label text for the new list or combo box.

8. Click **Finish**. Your new list or combo box appears on your form (see Figure 14.5).

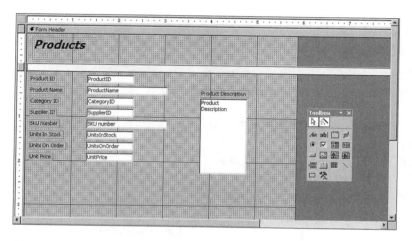

**FIGURE 14.5**
*Your list or combo box appears on the form grid.*

**CAUTION**

**Where Are My Values?**    Don't be alarmed that the values you entered for the control don't appear in the box in the Design view. The values will be available when you switch to the Form view and do data entry on the form.

**TIP**

**I Picked the Wrong Box Type!**    You can easily switch between a list box and a combo box, even after you create it. In Form Design view, right-click the control, click **Change To** from the shortcut menu that appears, and select a new control type.

## CREATING AN OPTION GROUP

Another useful special control is the *option group*. An option group provides different types of buttons or input boxes that can be used to quickly input information into a form. An option group can use one of the following types of buttons:

- **Option buttons**—A separate option button is provided for each choice you supply on the form. To make a particular choice, click the appropriate option button.

- **Check boxes**—A separate check box is provided for each item you place in the option group. To select a particular item, click the appropriate check box.

- **Toggle buttons**—A button is provided for the response required, which can be toggled on and off by clicking the button.

Option groups work best when a fairly limited number of choices is available, and when you create your option group, you should select the type of button or box that best suits your need. If you have several responses where only one response is valid, use option buttons. If you have a situation in which more than one response is possible, use check boxes. Toggle buttons are used when only one response is possible, and it responds to a yes or no type question. The option button is then turned on or off with a click of the mouse.

**TIP**

 **Other Options**    You can create a series of option buttons or check boxes using the Option Group button, or you can opt to directly create option buttons or check boxes by clicking the required button (the **Option** button or the **Check Box** button, respectively) on the Toolbox.

To create an Option Group control (you will create a control that uses option buttons), follow these steps:

1. Make sure that the **Control Wizards** button in the Toolbox is selected.

2. Click the **Option Group** button on the Toolbox. Your mouse pointer changes to show the Option Group icon.

3. Drag your mouse pointer on your form to draw a box where you want the option group to appear. When you release the mouse button, the wizard starts.

4. The wizard prompts you to enter the labels you want for each button (or check box or toggle button), as shown in Figure 14.6. You will need a label for each button that will appear in the group. These labels should be the same as the type of data you would normally insert into the field for which you are building the option group (which is specified in step 7). Enter the labels needed, pressing **Tab** after each one; then click **Next**.

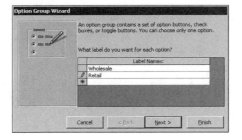

**FIGURE 14.6**
*Enter the labels you want for each option here.*

5. On the next screen, you can select one of the labels that you input in step 4 as the default choice for the option group. Specify the label, and then click **Yes, the Default Choice Is**. Or click **No, I Don't Want a Default As the Other Possibility**. Then click **Next**.

6. On the next screen, the wizard asks what value you want to assign to each option (such as 1, 2, and so on). These values provide a numerical equivalent for each label you listed in step 4 and are used by Access to store the response provided by a particular option button or check box. You should use the default values that Access provides. Click **Next** to continue.

7. On the next screen, you decide whether the value that you assigned to each of your option labels is stored in a particular field or saved by Access for later use. Because you are using the option group to input data into a particular field, be sure the **Store the Value in This Field** option button is selected. This stores the data that the option group provides in a particular field. Select the field from the drop-down list provided. Then, click **Next** to continue.

8. On the next screen, select the type of control (option button, check box, or toggle button—see Figure 14.7) you want to use and a style for the controls; then click **Next**.

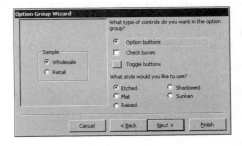

**FIGURE 14.7**
*You can choose different input controls for your Option group.*

9. On the last screen, type a label for the new control. Then click **Finish**.

Your new Option control appears on the grid area of the form. All the different option values that you entered appear in the control. When you switch to the Form view to enter data, you can use the various option buttons or check boxes to select an actual value for that particular field.

## ADDING COMMAND BUTTONS

Another special control type that you can add to your form is a command button. Command buttons are used to perform a particular action. For example, you could put a command button on a form that enables you to move to the next record or to print the form. Access offers different command button types that you can place on your forms:

- **Record Navigation**—You can add command buttons that allow you to move to the next, previous, first, or last record.

- **Record Operations**—You can make buttons that delete, duplicate, print, save, or undo a record.

- **Form Operations**—Command buttons can print a form, open a page (on a multiple page form), or close the form.

- **Application**—Command buttons can exit Access or run some other application.

- **Miscellaneous**—Command buttons can print a table, run a macro, run a query, or use the AutoDialer to dial a phone number specified on a form.

**TIP**

**Placing Command Button** Form headers or footers make a great place to put any command buttons that you create. Placing them in the header makes it easy for you to go to the top of the form and click a particular command button.

To place a command button on a form, follow these steps:

1. Be sure that the **Control Wizards** button in the Toolbox is selected.

 2. Click the **Command Button** in the Toolbox. Your mouse pointer changes to show the Command Button icon.

3. Click your form where you want the command button to appear (such as the header of the form). The Command Button Wizard opens.

4. On the first wizard screen, select an action category in the Categories list, and then in the Actions box (see Figure 14.8), select the action that the button should perform. Then click **Next**.

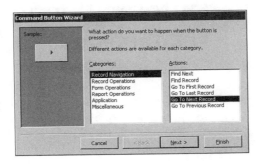

**FIGURE 14.8**
*Choose what action you want the command button to execute.*

5. On the next screen, you can select to have either text or a picture appear on the command button. For text, choose **Text** and then enter the text into the appropriate box. To place a picture on the button, select **Picture** and then select a picture from the list provided (you can use your own bitmap pictures on the buttons if they are available; use the **Browse** button to locate them). Then click **Next**.

6. On the next screen, type a name for your new button. Then click **Finish**. The button appears on your form. You can move it around like any other control.

In this lesson, you learned how to create list and combo boxes, option groups, and command buttons. In the next lesson, you learn how to search for data in a table and replace it with the Find and Replace features.

# LESSON 15

# Searching for Information in Your Database

*In this lesson, you learn how to search for data in a database using the Find feature and how to find and replace data using the Replace feature.*

## USING THE FIND FEATURE

Whether you are viewing the records in the table using the Datasheet view or a form, the Find feature is useful for locating a particular record in a table. For example, if you keep a database of customers, you might want to find a particular customer's record quickly by searching using the customer's last name. You can search the table using a specific field, or you can search the entire table (all the fields) for a certain text string.

Although the Find feature is designed to find information in a table, you can use the Find feature in both the Table Datasheet view and the Form view. The results of a particular search display only the first match of the parameters, but you can repeat the search to find additional records (one at a time).

**TIP**

> **Finding More Than One Record**   If you need to find several records at once, Find is not the best tool because it locates only one record at a time. A better tool for locating multiple records is a filter, discussed in the next lesson.

To find a particular record, follow these steps:

1. Open your table in the Datasheet view or open a form that is used to enter data in the table that you want to search.

2. Click in the field that contains the data for which you want to search.

3. Select **Edit**, **Find**, or press **Ctrl+F**. The Find and Replace dialog box appears (see Figure 15.1) with the Find tab on top.

**FIGURE 15.1**
*Use the Find and Replace dialog box to find data in a record.*

4. Type the data string that you want to find into the **Find What** text box.

5. The default value for Look In is the field you selected in step 2. If you want to search the entire table, click the **Look In** list drop-down box and select the table's name.

6. From the **Match** drop-down list, select one of the following:

   - **Whole Field**—Select this to find fields where the specified text is the only thing in that field. For example, "Smith" would not find "Smithsonian."

   - **Start of Field**—Select this to find fields that begin with the specified text. For example, "Smith" would find "Smith" and "Smithsonian," but not "Joe Smith."

   - **Any Part of Field**—Select this to find fields that contain the specified text in any way. "Smith" would find "Smith," "Smithsonian," and "Joe Smith."

7. To limit the match to entries that are the same case (upper-case or lowercase) as the search string, select the **Match Case** check box.

8. To find only fields with the same formatting as the text you type, select **Search Fields As Formatted** (this option can slow down the search on a large table, so don't use it unless you think it will affect the search results).

9. When you are ready to run the search, click **Find Next**.

10. If needed, move the Find and Replace dialog box out of the way by dragging its title bar so that you can see the record it found. If Access finds a field matching your search, it highlights the field entry containing the found text (see Figure 15.2).

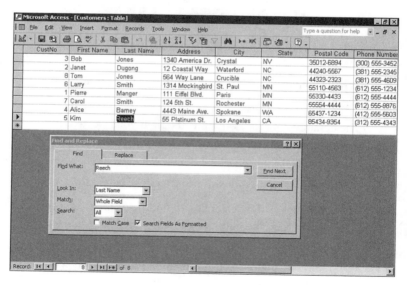

**FIGURE 15.2**

*Access finds records, one record at a time, that contain the search text.*

11. To find the next occurrence, click **Find Next**. If Access can't find any more occurrences, it tells you the search item was not found. Click **OK** to clear that message.

12. When you finish finding your data, click the Find and Replace dialog box **Close (X)** button.

## USING THE REPLACE FEATURE

The Replace feature is similar to the Find feature, except that you can stipulate that a value, which you specify, replace the data found during the search. For example, if you found that you misspelled a brand name or other value in a table, you could replace the word with the correct spelling. This is useful for correcting proper names because the Spelling Checker doesn't help correct those types of spelling errors.

To find and replace data, follow these steps:

1. Select **Edit**, **Replace**, or press **Ctrl+H**. The Find and Replace dialog box appears with the Replace tab displayed (see Figure 15.3).

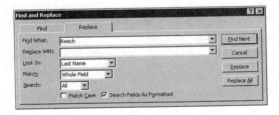

**FIGURE 15.3**
*You can find specific text in a table and then replace it using the Replace feature.*

2. Type the text you want to find into the **Find What** text box.

3. Type the text you want to replace it with into the **Replace With** text box.

4. Select any options you want using the Match drop-down list or the check boxes on the Search tab. They work the same as the options discussed on the Find tab (in the previous section).

5. To start the search, click **Find Next**. Access finds the first occurrence of the search string.

6. Click the **Replace** button to replace the text.

7. Click **Find Next** to find other occurrences, if desired, and replace them by clicking the **Replace** button.

8. If you decide that you would like to replace all occurrences of the search string in the table, click the **Replace All** button.

9. When you have found the last occurrence of the search string (Access lets you know that the string can no longer be located, which means you are at the end of the table), click the **Close** (x) button on the Find and Replace dialog box.

The Find and Replace feature works well when you want to work with data in a particular field, but it is limited because you can work with only one record at a time. Other, more sophisticated ways exist to locate records that contain a particular parameter. For example, you can filter records (discussed in the next lesson) using a particular field's content as the filter criteria. This provides you with a subset of the current table, showing you only the records that include the filter criteria.

Queries also provide you with a method for creating a subset of records found in a database table. Queries are discussed in Lesson 17, "Creating a Simple Query," and Lesson 18, "Creating Queries from Scratch."

In this lesson, you learned how to find and replace data in a database. In the next lesson, you learn how to sort, filter, and index records in a database table.

# LESSON 16
# Sorting, Filtering, and Indexing Data

*In this lesson, you learn how to find data by sorting and filtering and how to speed up searches with indexing.*

## FINDING AND ORGANIZING YOUR DATA

You've already had a chance to work with the Find and Replace features (in the previous lesson). Find and Replace are great features when you're working with individual instances of a particular value and want to search for it in a particular field. This lesson takes a look at other ways to organize the data in the table, including the Sort and Filter features.

## SORTING DATA

Although you probably entered your records into the table in some kind of logical order, perhaps by employee number or employee start date, being able to change the order of the records in the table based on a particular field parameter can be extremely useful. This is where the Sort feature comes in.

Using Sort, you can rearrange the records in the table based on any field in the table (more complex sorts can also be created that allow you to sort by more than one field, such as Last Name and then First Name). You can sort in either ascending (A to Z, 1 to 10) or descending (Z to A, 10 to 1) order.

## PLAIN ENGLISH

**Which View?**   You can sort either in Form view or Data-sheet view, but the Datasheet view is better because it shows you all the records in the table in their new sort order.

The fastest way to sort is to use either the **Sort Ascending** or **Sort Descending** button on the Table toolbar. However, this easy road to sorting limits you to sorting by one field or adjacent fields.

Follow these steps to sort records:

1. Place the insertion point in the field by which you want to sort the table (if you want to sort by more than one adjacent field, select the field columns by clicking and dragging the Field Column names). Figure 16.1 shows a Customers table where the insertion point has been placed in the Country field.

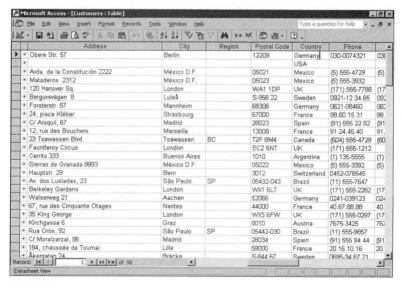

**FIGURE 16.1**
*Place the insertion point in the field by which you want to sort that table.*

2. To sort the records in the table by that field in ascending order (alphabetically from A to Z), click the **Sort Ascending** button. Figure 16.2 shows the results of an ascending sort by Country field on the table that was shown in Figure 16.1.

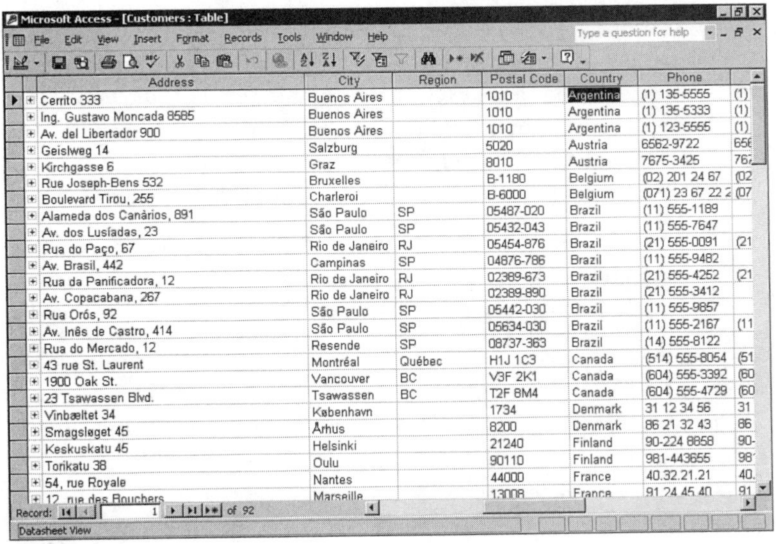

**FIGURE 16.2**
*The table records are sorted based on the field that you selected.*

3. To sort the records in descending order, click the **Sort Descending** button.

4. To place the records back in their presorted order, select the **Records** menu, and then select **Remove Filter/Sort**.

As already mentioned, you can sort a table by adjacent fields using the sort buttons. All you have to do is select the field headings for those particular field columns, and then click the correct sort button. For example, if you wanted to sort a customer table by last name and then first name, the last name would have to be in the column that is directly to the left of the First Name field.

## Filtering Data

Although sorting rearranges the records in the table, you might need to see a subset of the records in a table based on a particular criterion. Filtering is used for this purpose. The Filter feature temporarily hides records from the table that do not meet the filter criteria.

For example, you might want to view the records in an employee table where the employees have exceeded their sales goal for the year. Or in an order table, you might want to find orders that were placed on a particular date. Filters can help you temporarily narrow down the records shown in the table based on your criteria.

You can apply a filter in three ways: Filter by Selection (or Filter Excluding Selection), Filter by Form, and Advanced Filter/Sort. The first two methods are very easy ways to quickly filter the records in a table.

The Advanced Filter/Sort feature uses a Design view that is almost the same as the Query Design view (covered in Lesson 18, "Creating Queries from Scratch"). If you learn how to create queries (which are really nothing more than advanced filters/sorts), you will be able to work with the Advanced Filter/Sort feature.

This section covers Filter by Selection and Filter by Form. Next, take a look at how you filter by selection.

### Filter by Selection

Filtering by selection is the easiest method of filtering, but before you can use it, you must locate a field that contains the value that you want to use to filter the table. For example, if you want to filter a customer table by a country, such as Germany, you must locate a field in a record that contains the text "Germany."

To filter by selection, follow these steps:

1. Locate a field in a record that contains the value you want to use to filter the table. For example, if you want to see all the customers in Germany, you would find a field in the Country field column that contains "Germany."

2. Select the data in the field.

3. Click the **Filter by Selection** button on the toolbar, or select **Records**, point at **Filter**, and then choose **Filter by Selection**. The records that match the criteria you selected appear as shown in Figure 16.3.

**TIP**

> **Fine-Tuning Filter by Selection**   You can also filter the table by selecting only a portion of an entry in a field. For example, if you want to filter the records by last names beginning with the letter S, select the S in a last name that appears in the Last Name field in a record.

| Address | City | Region | Postal Code | Country | Phone | |
|---|---|---|---|---|---|---|
| Obere Str. 57 | Berlin | | 12209 | Germany | 030-0074321 | 030-0 |
| Forsterstr. 57 | Mannheim | | 68306 | Germany | 0621-08460 | 0621- |
| Walserweg 21 | Aachen | | 52066 | Germany | 0241-039123 | 0241- |
| Berliner Platz 43 | München | | 80805 | Germany | 089-0877310 | 089-0 |
| Maubelstr. 90 | Brandenburg | | 14776 | Germany | 0555-09876 | |
| Magazinweg 7 | Frankfurt a.M. | | 60528 | Germany | 069-0245984 | 069-0 |
| Heerstr. 22 | Leipzig | | 04179 | Germany | 0342-023176 | |
| Mehrheimerstr. 369 | Köln | | 50739 | Germany | 0221-0644327 | 0221- |
| Taucherstraße 10 | Cunewalde | | 01307 | Germany | 0372-035188 | |
| Luisenstr. 48 | Münster | | 44087 | Germany | 0251-031259 | 0251- |
| Adenauerallee 900 | Stuttgart | | 70563 | Germany | 0711-020361 | 0711- |

**FIGURE 16.3**
*The table will be filtered by the field data you selected.*

With Filter by Selection, you can filter by only one criterion at a time. However, you can apply successive filters after the first one to further narrow the list of matching records.

You can also filter for records that don't contain the selected value. Follow the same steps as outlined in this section, but choose **Records**, point at **Filter**, and choose **Filter Excluding Selection** in step 3.

After you have finished viewing the records that match your filter criteria, you will want to bring all the table records back on screen. Select **Records, Remove Filter/Sort**.

## FILTER BY FORM

Filtering by form is a more powerful filtering method than filtering by selection. With Filter by Form, you can filter by more than one criterion at a time. To filter by form, follow these steps:

1. With the table open in the Datasheet view, click the **Filter by Form** button on the toolbar, or select **Records**, point at **Filter**, and then select **Filter by Form**. A blank form appears, resembling an empty datasheet with a single record line.

2. Click in the field for which you want to set a criterion. A down arrow appears for a drop-down list. Click the arrow and select the value you want from the list (see Figure 16.4). You also can type the value directly into the field if you prefer.

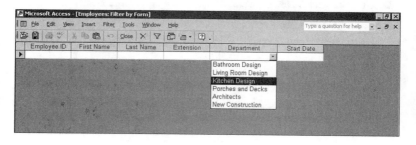

**FIGURE 16.4**
*Set the criteria for the filter using the drop-down list in each field.*

3. Enter additional criteria for the filter as needed using the drop-down lists provided by the other fields in the table.

4. After you enter your criteria, click the **Apply Filter** button on the toolbar. Your filtered data appears in the Table window.

As in Filter by Selection, you can remove a filter by clicking the **Remove Filter** button or by selecting **Records, Remove Filter/Sort**.

## SAVING YOUR FILTER AS A QUERY

If you design a filter that you would like to keep, you can save it as a query. After it is saved as a query, it resides on the Query list in the database window. You will work with queries in Lessons 17 and 18.

To save a filter as a query, follow these steps:

1. Display the filter in Filter by Form view.

2. Select **File**, **Save As Query**. Access asks for the name of the new query.

3. Type a name and click **OK**. Access saves the filter as a query.

# INDEXING DATA

Although not a method of manipulating data like a sort or a filter, indexes provide a method for speeding up searches, sorts, and filters by cataloging the contents of a particular field. The primary key field in a table is automatically indexed. If you have a large database table and frequently search, sort, or filter by a field other than the primary key field, you might want to create an index for that field.

 **CAUTION**

**Can't Be Indexed**   You can't index a field whose data type is Memo, Hyperlink, or OLE Object. There is no way for Access to verify the content of fields containing these types of entries, making it impossible to create an index.

To index a field, follow these steps:

1. Open the table in Design view.

2. Select the field that you want to index.

3. In the Field Properties pane on the General tab, click in the **Indexed** box.

4. From the Indexed field's drop-down list, select either **Yes (Duplicates OK)** or **Yes (No Duplicates)**, depending on whether that field's content should be unique for each record (see Figure 16.5). For example, in the case of indexing a last name field, you would want to allow duplicates (Duplicates OK), but in the case of a Social Security number field where you know each entry is unique, you would not want to allow duplicates (No Duplicates).

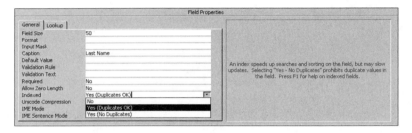

**FIGURE 16.5**
*To index a field, set its Indexed value to one of the Yes choices.*

5. Save your changes to the table's structure by clicking the **Save** button on the Design toolbar.

6. Close the Design view of the table.

Indexes aren't glamorous. They work behind the scenes to speed up your searches and filters. They don't really have any independent functions of their own.

In this lesson, you learned how to sort, filter, and index your database tables. In the next lesson, you learn how to create a query using the Query Wizard.

# LESSON 17
# Creating a Simple Query

*In this lesson, you create a simple query.*

## UNDERSTANDING QUERIES

As you learned in the previous lesson, Access offers many ways to help you narrow down the information you're looking at, including sorting and filtering. The most flexible way to sort and filter data, however, is using a query.

A *query* is a question that you pose to a database table or tables. For example, you might want to know which of your customers live in a specific state or how many of your salespeople have reached a particular sales goal. The great thing about queries is that you can save queries and use them to create tables, delete records, or copy records to another table.

Queries enable you to specify

- The table fields that appear in the query

- The order of the fields in the query

- Filter and sort criteria for each field in the query

### PLAIN ENGLISH

> **Query**   A query enables you to "question" your database using different criteria that can sort, filter, and summarize table data.

Queries are a powerful tool for analyzing and summarizing database information. In this lesson, you take a look at the queries you can create using a wizard. Creating queries in the Design view is covered in Lesson 18, "Creating Queries from Scratch."

## USING THE SIMPLE QUERY WIZARD

The easiest way to create a query is with the Simple Query Wizard, which enables you to select the table fields you want to include in the query. A simple query is useful when you want to weed out extraneous fields but still want to see every record in the database table. The Simple Query Wizard helps you create a *select query*.

**PLAIN ENGLISH**

**Select Query**    The select query is used to select certain data from a table or tables. It not only filters the data, but it can also sort the data. It can even perform simple calculations on the results (such as counting and averaging).

To create a select query with the Simple Query Wizard, follow these steps:

1. In the Access window, open the database with which you want to work and select the **Queries** icon in the database window.

2. Double-click **Create Query by Using Wizard**. The first dialog box of the Simple Query Wizard appears (see Figure 17.1).

3. Choose the table from which you want to select fields from the Tables/Queries drop-down list.

4. Click a field name in the Available Fields list; then click the **Add (>)** button to move the field name to the Selected Fields list. Add fields as needed, or move them all at once with the **Add All (>>)** button.

5. (Optional) Select another table or query from the Tables/Queries list and add some of its fields to the Selected Fields list (this enables you to pull data from more than one table into the query). When you have finished adding fields, click **Next**.

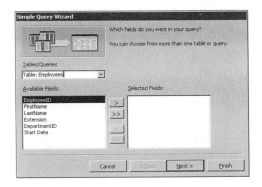

**FIGURE 17.1**
*The Simple Query Wizard first asks what fields you want to include in the query.*

**CAUTION**

**Relationships Required**    If you're going to use two or more tables in your query, they must be joined by a relationship. See Lesson 11, "Creating Relationships Between Tables," for more information.

6. On the next screen, enter a title for the query. Then, click **Finish** to view the query results. Figure 17.2 shows the results of a simple query.

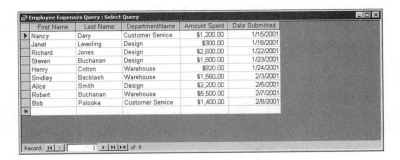

**FIGURE 17.2**
*Queries created using the Simple Query Wizard list the data from the fields you selected.*

The problem with queries created using the Simple Query Wizard is that you aren't supplied with the option of setting sort parameters for the records or the capability to filter them by particular criteria. Simple queries just allow you to select the fields. For this query to provide a little more manipulation of the table data, you would have to edit this Query Design view, which is discussed in the next lesson. Building queries from scratch provides you with a lot more control over how the data is filtered, sorted, and summarized.

## Saving a Query

When you create a query, Access saves it automatically. You don't need to do anything special to save it. When you are finished viewing the results of the query, click its **Close (x)** button. The new query is then listed in the Query list that the database window provides.

## Rerunning a Query

At any time, you can rerun your query. If the data has changed in the table fields that you included in a query, rerunning the query provides you with an updated set of results.

To rerun a query, follow these steps:

1. Open the database containing the query.

2. Select the **Queries** icon in the database window.

3. In the Query list, double-click the query you want to run, or click it once and then click the **Open** button.

 **TIP**

> **Queries Look Like Tables**   Queries can be manipulated in the Datasheet view just like a table. You can use the Sort and Filter features on a query, or you can delete records from the query.

# USING OTHER QUERY WIZARDS

Access's different query features are quite powerful; they can do amazingly complicated calculations and comparisons on data from several tables. Queries also can do calculations to summarize data or arrange the query data in a special format called a crosstab. Creating more advanced queries means that your database tables must be joined by the appropriate relationships; otherwise, the query cannot pull the data from multiple tables.

You can create very complex queries from the Query Design view, which you learn about in the next lesson. However, Access also provides some wizards that can be used to create some of the more complex query types. These wizards include the following:

- **Crosstab Query Wizard**—This wizard displays summarized values, such as sums, counts, and averages, from a field. One field is used on the left side of the Query datasheet to cross-reference other field columns in the Query datasheet. For example, Figure 17.3 shows a Crosstab table that displays the different products that a customer has ordered, sorted on the customer's first name.

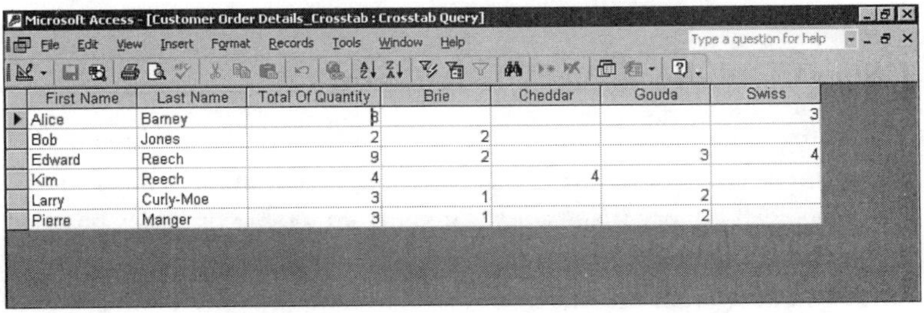

**FIGURE 17.3**
*Crosstab queries allow you to cross-tabulate information between table fields.*

- **Find Duplicates Query Wizard**—This query is used to compare two tables and find duplicate records.

• **Find Unmatched Query Wizard**—This wizard compares two tables and finds all records that don't appear in both tables (based on comparing certain fields).

You can access any of these query wizards from the database window. With the Query icon selected, click the **New** button on the database window toolbar. The New Query dialog box appears, as shown in Figure 17.4.

**FIGURE 17.4**
*The other query wizards can be accessed from the New Query dialog box.*

Select the wizard that you want to use for your query and click **OK**. Work with the wizard as it walks you through the steps for creating your new query.

## UNDERSTANDING ACCESS QUERY TYPES

Before this lesson ends, you should spend a little time learning about the different types of queries that Access offers. In this lesson, you created a select query that "selects" data from a table or tables based on your query criteria. You can also build other types of queries. The different query types are

• **Make Table Query**—This type of query is similar to a select query, but it takes the data pulled together by the criteria and creates a new table for the database.

• **Update Query**—This query updates field information in a record. For example, you might have placed a certain credit limit for customers and want to update it in all the records. You would use an Update query.

- **Append Query**—This type of query is used to copy records from one table and place them (append them) into another table. For example, you might want to append employee records from an Active Employee table to a Former Employee table.

- **Delete Query**—This type of query is used to delete records from a table. For example, you might want to delete old records from a table based on particular criteria.

Now, you might be thinking that all these query types are a little too much to handle. However, you create different query types just as you would a select query.

As a matter of fact, you actually design each of these different query types as a select table (using a wizard, Query Design view, or a combination of both), and then you change the query type in the Query Design view. It's just a matter of selecting the query type from the Query menu.

In this lesson, you learned how to create a simple query and how to save, edit, and print query results. You also learned about the different query wizards and the different types of queries. In the next lesson you work in the Query Design view.

# LESSON 18

# Creating Queries from Scratch

*In this lesson, you learn how to open a query in Design view, how to select fields to include in it, and how to specify criteria for filtering the records.*

## INTRODUCING QUERY DESIGN VIEW

In Lesson 17, "Creating a Simple Query," you created a simple query using the Simple Query Wizard. This wizard allowed you to select the fields from a particular table and then create a standard select query. Although the Simple Query Wizard makes it easy to create a query based on one table, you will find that building more sophisticated queries is best done in the Query Design view.

The Query Design view provides two distinct areas as you work. A Table pane shows you the tables currently being used for the query. The bottom pane, the Query Design grid (see Figure 18.1) enables you to list the fields in the query and select how these fields will be sorted or the information in them filtered when you run the query.

### OPENING A QUERY IN QUERY DESIGN VIEW

One thing that you can do in the Query Design view is edit existing queries, such as the simple query that you created in the previous lesson. You can change the fields used in the query and change the action that takes place on that field (or fields) when you run the query. To open an existing query in Query Design view, follow these steps:

1. Open the database that contains the query you want to edit (select **File, Open**).

2. In the database window, click the **Queries** icon.

3. In the Query list, select the query you want to edit.

4. Click the **Design** button on the database window toolbar.

The query opens in the Query Design window.

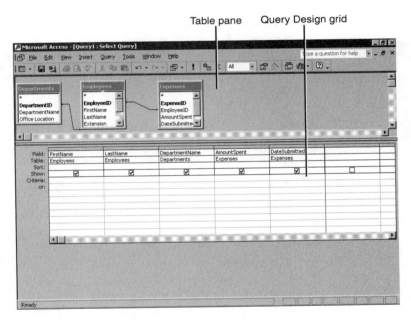

**FIGURE 18.1**
*The Query Design view is divided into a Table pane and a Query Design grid.*

## Starting a New Query in Query Design View

Creating a new query from scratch in the Query Design view allows you to select both the tables and the fields that you use to build the query. To begin a new query in Query Design view, follow these steps:

1. Open the database that holds the table or tables that you will use to build the query.

2. Click the **Queries** icon in the database window.

3. In the Query list, double-click **Create Query in Design View**. The Show Table dialog box appears, listing all the tables in the database (see Figure 18.2).

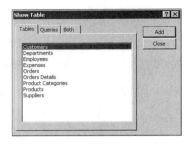

**FIGURE 18.2**
*Choose which tables you want to include in the query.*

4. Click a table that contains fields you want to use in the query, and then click the **Add** button. Repeat for each table you want to add.

5. Click **Close** when you finish adding tables. The Query Design view window opens.

The tables chosen for the query appear in the top pane of the Query Design view. Field names do not appear in the Query Design grid until you add them. Adding fields to the query is covered in the next section.

**PLAIN ENGLISH**

**Create Table Relationships** When you create queries from multiple tables, these tables must be related. See Lesson 11, "Creating Relationships Between Tables" for more information.

## Adding Fields to a Query

Whether you create your query from scratch or modify an existing query, the Query Design view provides the capability to add the table fields that will be contained in the query. Be sure that the tables that contain the fields for the query are present in the design window.

**TIP**

> **Adding More Tables**    You can add tables to your query at any time. Click the **Show Table** button on the toolbar, or select **Query, Show Table**. Then, select the tables you want and click **Add**. Click **Close** to return to your query design.

To add a field to the query, follow these steps:

1. In the first field column of the query grid, click in the **Field** box. A drop-down arrow list appears.

2. Click the drop-down list and select a field (see Figure 18.3). Because all the fields available in the tables you selected for the query are listed, you might have to scroll down through the list to find the field you want to use.

3. Click in the next field column and repeat the procedure. Add the other fields that you want to include in the query as needed.

As you add the fields to the query from left to right, be advised that this will be the order in which the fields appear in the query when you run it. If you need to change the field that you've placed in a particular field column, use the Field drop-down list in the column to select a different field.

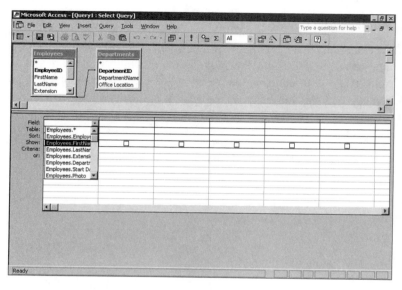

**FIGURE 18.3**
*Scroll through the Field list to locate the field you want to place in the query.*

**TIP**

> **Quickly Add Fields to the Query**　You can also add fields to
> the query directly from the tables that appear in the Table
> pane of the Query Design view. In one of the tables,
> locate the field that you want to place in the first field
> column and double-click the field name (in the table
> itself). The field appears in the Field box in the first field
> column of the query grid. To add the next field, locate it
> in a table, and then double-click it. This method enables
> you to select the fields from specific tables rather than
> scrolling through a long, continuous list of field names.

## DELETING A FIELD

If you place a field that you don't want into a field column, you can
replace it using the drop-down list in the Field box (of that column) to
select a different field. If you don't want a field in that field column at

all, you can delete the field from the query. Deleting the field deletes the entire field column from the query. You can use two methods for deleting a field column from the query:

- Click anywhere in the column and select **Edit, Delete Columns**.

- Position the mouse pointer directly above the column so that the pointer turns into a downward-pointing black arrow. Then click to select the entire column. To delete the selected field column, press **Delete**.

After you have the fields selected that you will use in the table, you are ready to set the criteria for the query.

## ADDING CRITERIA

The criteria that you set for your query determines how the field information found in the selected fields appears in the completed query. You set criteria in the query to filter the field data. The criteria that you set in a query are similar to the criteria that you worked with when you used the filtering features in Lesson 16, "Sorting, Filtering, and Indexing Data."

For example, suppose you have a query where you have selected fields from an Employee table and a Department table (which are related tables in your company database). The query lists the employees and their departments. You would also like to list only employees that were hired before March 1999. This means that you would set a criteria for your Start Date field of <03/01/99. Using the less-than sign (<) simply tells Access that you want the query to filter out employee records where the start date is before (less than) March 1, 1999.

To set criteria for a field in your query, follow these steps:

1. In Query Design view, click the **Criteria** row in the desired field's column.

2. Type the criteria you want to use (see Figure 18.4).

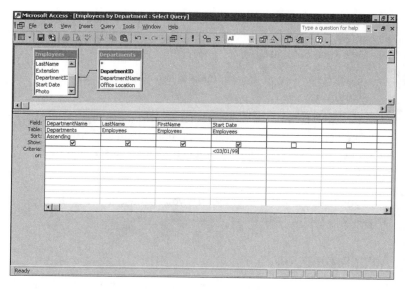

**FIGURE 18.4**
Enter your criteria into the Criteria row of the appropriate field's column.

**3.** Queries can contain multiple criteria. Repeat steps 1 and 2 as needed to add additional criteria to field columns in the query.

Query criteria can act both on alphanumeric field data (text) and numeric data (dates are seen by Access as numerical information). For example, suppose you have a Customer table that lists customers in two states: Ohio (OH) and Pennsylvania (PA). Criteria used to filter the customer data in a query so that only customers in PA are shown in the query results would be PA. It's that simple.

When you work with criteria, symbols are used (such as the less-than sign that appears in the criteria in Figure 18.4) to specify how the query should react to the data string that you place in the Criteria box. Table 18.1 provides a list of some of these symbols and what you use them for.

**Table 18.1**  Sample Criteria for Queries

| Symbol | Used For |
| --- | --- |
| < (less than) | Matching values must be less than (or before in the case of dates) the specified numerical string. |
| > (greater than) | Matching values must be greater than (or after in the case of dates) the specified numerical string. |
| <= (less than or equal to) | Matching values must be equal to or less than the value used in the criteria. |
| >= (greater than or equal to) | Matching values must be equal to or greater than the value used in the criteria. |
| = (equal to) | Matching values must be equal to the criteria string. This symbol can be used both with text and numeric entries. |
| Not | Values matching the criteria string will not be included in the results. For example, Not PA filters out all the records in which PA is in the state field. |

## USING THE TOTAL ROW IN A QUERY

You can also do calculations in a query, such as totaling numeric information in a particular field or taking the average of numeric information found in a particular field in the query. To add calculations to a query, you must add the Total row to the Query Design grid.

After the Total row is available in the query grid, different calculations can be chosen from a drop-down list in any of the fields that you have chosen for the query. For example, you can sum (total) the numeric information in a field, calculate the average, and even do more intense statistical analysis with formulas such as minimum, maximum, and standard deviation.

To add a calculation to a field in the query grid, follow these steps:

1. In Query Design view, click the **Totals** button on the Query Design toolbar. The Total row is added to the Query Design grid (just below the Table row).

2. Click in the Total row for a field in the Query Design grid that contains numerical information. A drop-down arrow appears.

3. Click the drop-down arrow (see Figure 18.5) to select the formula you want to place in the field's Total box. The following are some of the more commonly used formula expressions:

   - **Sum**—Totals the values found in the field.

   - **Avg**—Calculates the average for the values found in the field.

   - **Min**—Displays the lowest value (the minimum) found in the field.

   - **Max**—Displays the highest value (the maximum) found in the field.

   - **Count**—Calculates the number of entries in the field; it actually "counts" the entries.

   - **StDev**—Calculates the standard deviation for the values in the field. The standard deviation calculates how widely values in the field differ from the field's average value.

4. Repeat steps 2 and 3 to place formulas into other field columns.

When you use the Total row, you can summarize the information in a particular field mathematically when you run the query. For example, you might want to total the number of orders for a particular product, so you would use the sum formula provided by the Total drop-down list.

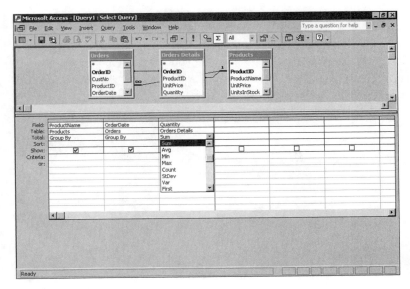

**FIGURE 18.5**
*Calculations added to the Total row are chosen from a drop-down list.*

## VIEWING QUERY RESULTS

After you have selected the fields for the query and have set your field criteria, you are ready to run the query. As with tables created in the Design view and forms created in the Design view, you should save the query after you have finished designing it.

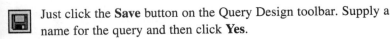 Just click the **Save** button on the Query Design toolbar. Supply a name for the query and then click **Yes**.

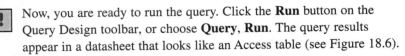 Now, you are ready to run the query. Click the **Run** button on the Query Design toolbar, or choose **Query, Run**. The query results appear in a datasheet that looks like an Access table (see Figure 18.6).

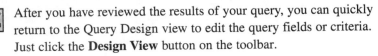 After you have reviewed the results of your query, you can quickly return to the Query Design view to edit the query fields or criteria. Just click the **Design View** button on the toolbar.

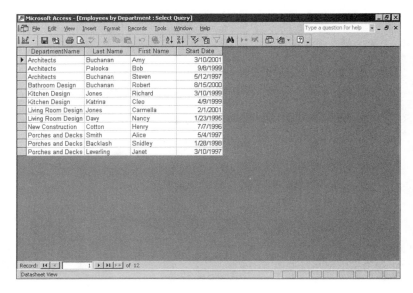

**FIGURE 18.6**
*The results of the query appear as a table datasheet.*

In this lesson, you learned how to choose the fields for a query and specify criteria in the Query Design view. In the next lesson, you learn how to create reports in Access by using the AutoReport feature and the Report Wizard.

# LESSON 19
# Creating a Simple Report

*In this lesson, you learn how to create reports in Access by using the
AutoReport feature and the Report Wizard.*

## UNDERSTANDING REPORTS

So far, the discussion of Access objects has centered on objects that
are used either to input data or manipulate data that has already been
entered into a table. Tables and forms provide different ways of entering records into the database, and queries enable you to sort and filter
the data in the database.

Now you are going to turn your attention to a database object that is
designed to summarize data and provide a printout of your database
information—an Access report. Reports are designed specifically to be
printed and shared with other people.

You can create a report in several ways, ranging from easy to difficult.
An AutoReport, the simplest possibility, takes all the records in a table
and provides a summary that is ready to print. The Report Wizard, an
intermediate possibility, is still simple to use but requires more deci-
sions on your part to select the fields and the structure of the report.
Finally, the most difficult method of creating a report is building a
report from scratch in the Report Design view. You learn about the
Report Design view in the next lesson.

## USING AUTOREPORT TO CREATE A REPORT

The fastest way to take data in a table and get it into a format that is
appropriate for printing is AutoReport. The AutoReport feature can

create a report in a tabular or columnar format. A tabular report resembles a datasheet in that it arranges the data from left to right on the page. A columnar report resembles a form in that it displays each record in the table from top to bottom. The downside of AutoReport is that it can create a report from only one table or query.

To use the AutoReport feature to create a simple report, follow these steps:

1. Open the database containing the table or query that you will use to create the report.

2. Click the **Reports** icon in the left pane of the database window.

3. Click the **New** button on the database toolbar. The New Report dialog box appears (see Figure 19.1).

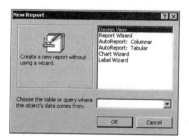

**FIGURE 19.1**
*Choose one of the AutoReport formats in the New Report dialog box.*

4. Select **AutoReport:Columnar** or **AutoReport:Tabular**.

5. In the drop-down list at the bottom of the dialog box, select the table or query on which you want to base the report.

6. Click **OK**. The report appears in Print Preview. The Print Preview mode allows you to examine your report before printing. You learn more about Print Preview later in this lesson.

**TIP**

 **Create an AutoReport from an Open Table**   You can also create an AutoReport directly from an open table. With the table open in the Access window, click the **New Object** drop-down list on the Table Datasheet toolbar and select AutoReport. This creates a simple columnar report.

AutoReport produces fairly simple-looking reports. To have more control over the report format and layout, you can create a report using the Report Wizard.

## CREATING A REPORT WITH THE REPORT WIZARD

The Report Wizard offers a good compromise between ease-of-use and control over the report that is created. With the Report Wizard, you can build a report that uses multiple tables or queries. You can also choose a layout and format for the report. Follow these steps to create a report with Report Wizard:

1. Open the database containing the table or query on which you want to report.

2. Click the **Reports** icon in the database window.

3. In the Reports pane of the database window, double-click **Create Report by Using Wizard** to start the Report Wizard (see Figure 19.2). The first wizard screen enables you to choose the fields to include in the report.

4. From the Tables/Queries drop-down list, select a table or query from which you want to include fields.

5. Click a field in the Available Fields list, and then click the **Add** (>) button to move it to the Selected Fields list. Repeat this step to select all the fields you want, or click **Add All** (>>) to move all the fields over at once.

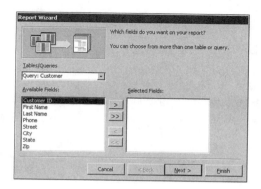

**FIGURE 19.2**
*The first Report Wizard screen enables you to select the fields for the report.*

6. For a report using fields from multiple tables, select another table or query from the Tables/Queries list and repeat step 5. To build the report from more than one table, you must create a relationship between the tables. When you finish selecting fields, click **Next** to continue.

7. On the next wizard screen, Access gives you the option of viewing the data by a particular category of information. The wizard provides this option only when you build a report from multiple tables. For example, if you have a report that includes fields from a Customer table, a Products table, and an Orders table, the information in the report can be organized either by customer, product, or order information (see Figure 19.3). Select the viewpoint for the data from the list on the left of the wizard screen; then select **Next** to continue.

8. On the next wizard screen, you can further group records in the report by a particular field. To group by a field, click the field and then click the > button. You can select several grouping levels in the order you want them. Then click **Next** to move on.

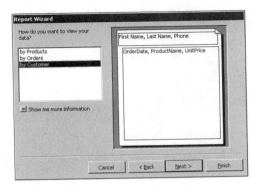

**FIGURE 19.3**
*Data in the report can be arranged from a particular viewpoint based on the tables used to create the report.*

**PLAIN ENGLISH**

**Grouping?**  By default, the field data in the report are not grouped. By selecting different group levels, you can group information by department, product, or any field that you select. Grouping the data enables you to create a report that has been divided into logical subsections.

9. The wizard asks whether you would like to sort the records in the report (see Figure 19.4). If you want to sort the records by a particular field or fields (you can sort by more than one field, such as by last name and then first name), open the top drop-down list and select a field by which to sort. From the drop-down lists, select up to four fields to sort by, and then click **Next**.

10. On the next wizard screen, choose a layout option  from the Layout section. When you click an option button for a particular layout, the sample in the box changes to show your selection.

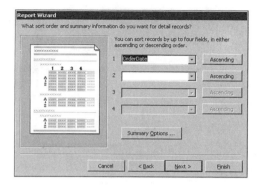

**FIGURE 19.4**
*Set the sort order for your records.*

**PLAIN ENGLISH**

**Where Are All the Layouts?** If you don't choose any group-ings in your report, you are limited to three layout choices: Columnar, Tabular, and Justified. More layouts are avail-able when you have set grouping options for the report.

11. In the next wizard dialog box, choose a report style. Several are listed; click one to see a sample of it, and then click **Next** when you're satisfied with your choice.

12. On the last wizard screen, you're asked for a report title. Enter one into the Report text box, and click **Finish** to see your report in Print Preview.

## VIEWING AND PRINTING REPORTS IN PRINT PREVIEW

When you create a report with either AutoReport or the Report Wizard, the report appears in Print Preview (as shown in Figure 19.5). From there, you can print the report if you're happy with it or go to Report Design view to make changes. (You'll learn more about the Report Design view in Lesson 20, "Customizing a Report.")

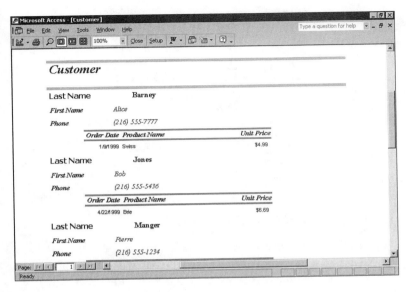

**FIGURE 19.5**
*Either AutoReports or reports created with the wizard automatically open in Print Preview.*

 In the Print Preview mode, you can zoom in and out on the report using the **Zoom** tool (click once to zoom in and click again to zoom out). Using the appropriate button on the Print Preview toolbar, you can also display the report as one page, two pages, or multiple pages.

 If you want to print the report and specify any print options (such as the number of copies), choose **File**, **Print**. If you want a quick hard copy, click the toolbar's **Print** button.

If you click the **Close** (**x**) button on the Print Preview toolbar, you are taken directly to the Report Design view. You learn about the Report Design view in the next lesson.

In this lesson, you learned how to create an AutoReport and a report using the Report Wizard. You also learned how to use Print Preview and print the report. In the next lesson, you learn how to work in Report Design view to customize your report.

# Lesson 20

# Customizing a Report

*In this lesson, you learn how to use Report Design view to make your reports more attractive.*

## ENTERING REPORT DESIGN VIEW

You've already seen that you can create reports using AutoReport and the Report Wizard. After you've created a report using either of these methods, you can edit or enhance the report in the Report Design view. You can also create Reports from scratch in the Report Design view.

The Report Design view is similar to the Form Design view that you worked with in Lesson 13, "Modifying a Form," and Lesson 14, "Adding Special Controls to Forms." Like forms, reports are made up of controls that are bound to fields in a table or tables in the database.

To edit an existing report in the Design view, follow these steps:

1. Click the **Reports** icon in the database window.

2. In the list of reports provided, select the report you want to modify.

3. Click the **Design** button on the database toolbar. The report appears in Design view, as shown in Figure 20.1.

As you can see in Figure 20.1, the report's underlying structure contains several areas. The Detail area contains the actual controls that relate to the table fields included in the report. Above the Detail area is the Page Header, which contains the labels that are associated with the controls in the Detail area. At the very top of the report is the Report Header. It contains a text box that displays the name of the report.

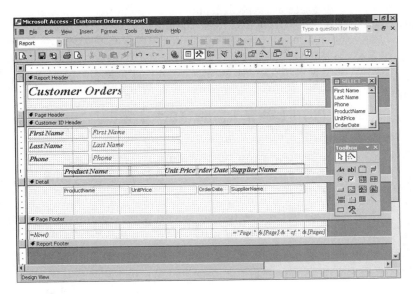

**FIGURE 20.1**
*The report is divided into several areas in the Design view.*

At the bottom of the report are two footers. The Page Footer contains formulas that display the current date and print the page number of the report. At the very bottom of the report is the Report Footer. The Report Footer is blank in Figure 20.1. It can be used, however, to insert a summary formula or other calculation that works with the data that appears in the Detail area (you will add a calculation to a report later in the lesson).

As already mentioned, the Report Design view is similar to Form Design view. The Report Design view also supplies the Toolbox, which is used to add text boxes and special controls to the report. The Field list allows you to add field controls to the report.

**CAUTION**

> **Using Special Controls on a Report**    Access enables you to place any type of control on a report, even command buttons or combo boxes. These won't do you much good on a report, however. It's better to stick to text boxes, labels, and graphics on reports—items that enhance the overall look of the report when it is printed.

## WORKING WITH CONTROLS ON YOUR REPORT

Working with report controls in Report Design view is the same as working with controls in Form Design view. You might want to turn back to Lesson 11 to review how you manipulate controls and their labels. The following is a brief review:

- **Selecting Controls**—Click the control to select it. Selection handles appear around the control.

- **Moving Objects**—To move a control, first select it. Next, position the mouse pointer over a border so that the pointer turns into an open hand. Then, click and drag the control to a new location.

**PLAIN ENGLISH**

> **Moving Between Report Areas**    You can't drag a control from one section of the report to another, but if you do need to move it, you can use cut and paste. Select the control (or label) and press **Ctrl+X** to cut it. Then, click the title of the section where you want to move it and press **Ctrl+V** to paste it into the newly selected section.

- **Resizing Objects**—First, select the object. Then, position the mouse pointer over a selection handle and drag it to resize the object.

- **Formatting Text Objects**—Use the **Font** and **Font Size** drop-down lists on the toolbar to choose fonts; then use the **Bold**, **Italic**, and **Underline** toolbar buttons to set special attributes.

You can add any controls to the report that the Toolbox provides. For example, you might want to add a graphic to the report, such as a company logo. The next section discusses adding an image to a report.

## ADDING AN IMAGE TO A REPORT

You can add graphics, clip art, or even images from a digital camera to your Access reports. For example, if you want to add a company logo to a report, all you need is access to the logo image file on your computer (or a company's network). If you want to include an image, such as a company logo, on the very first page of the report, you will want to add it to the Report Header. Any information or graphics placed in the Report Header will appear at the very top of the report. Images that you want to use to illustrate information in the report should go in the Details area.

To add an image to a report, follow these steps:

1. Expand the area of the report (such as the Report Header) in which you want to place the image. For example, to expand the Report Header, drag the Page Header's title bar downward using the mouse (the mouse becomes a sizing tool when you place it on an area's border).

2. Click the **Image** button on the Toolbox. The mouse pointer becomes an image drawing tool.

3. Drag to create a box or rectangle that will contain the image in the appropriate area of the report. When you release the mouse, the Insert Picture dialog box appears (see Figure 20.2).

4. Use the Look In drop-down list to locate the drive that contains the image file, and then open the appropriate folder by double-clicking.

**FIGURE 20.2**
*Use the Insert Picture dialog box to locate and insert your picture into the report.*

   5. When you locate your image, click the filename to select it, and then click **OK**. The image is inserted into the report.

You might find that the image file is larger than the image control that you have created. To make the image fit into the control, right-click the Image control and select **Properties** from the shortcut menu that appears. In the Properties dialog box, select the **Format** tab. Then, click in the Size Mode box and select **Zoom** from the drop-down list. This automatically sizes the graphic to fit into the control (which means that it typically shrinks the image to fit into the control). You can then close the Properties box.

**TIP**

> **Check Your Report Design in Print Preview**   As you work on the structure of your report in the Design view, you can check to see how things will look by switching to the Print Preview mode. Click the **Print Preview** button on the Report Design toolbar.

## ARRANGING AND REMOVING CONTROLS

As already mentioned, you can move or resize the controls on the report. This also goes for any new controls that you add from the Toolbox or by using the Field list. You can also remove unwanted controls from the report.

To delete a control, select it by clicking it, and then press **Delete**. Deleting a control from the report doesn't delete the field from the associated table.

## ADDING TEXT LABELS

You can also add descriptive labels to your report. For example, you might want to add a text box containing descriptive text to the Report Header.

 Click the **Label** button on the Toolbox. The mouse pointer becomes a label drawing tool. Drag with the mouse to create a text box in any of the areas on the report. When you release the mouse, you can begin typing the text that will be contained in the text label.

# PLACING A CALCULATION IN THE REPORT

Controls (also called text boxes in a report) most commonly display data from fields, as you've seen in the reports that you have created. However, text boxes can also hold calculations based on values in different fields.

Creating a text box is a bit complicated: First, you must create an unbound control/text box (that is, one that's not associated with any particular field), and then you must type the calculation into the text box. Follow these steps:

1. Click the **Text Box** tool in the Toolbox, and then click and drag on the report to create a text box.

2. Change the label to reflect what's going in the text box. For example, if it's sales tax or the total of your orders multiplied

by the price of your various products, change the label accordingly. Position the label where you want it.

3. Click in the text box and type the formula that you want calculated. (See the following list for guidance.)

4. Click anywhere outside the text box when you finish.

Figure 20.3 shows a control that provides the total value of the orders for each item. This control multiplies the Quantity control (which is tied to a field that supplies the number of orders for each item) by the UnitPrice control (which provides the price of each item).

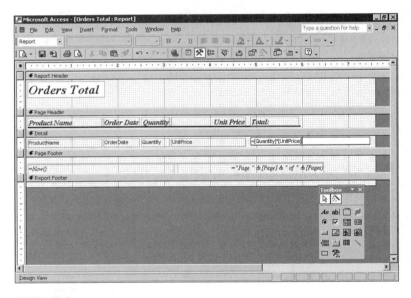

**FIGURE 20.3**
*You can add controls to the report that do math.*

The formulas you enter into your calculated text box use standard mathematical symbols:

+    Add

-    Subtract

\*       Multiply

/       Divide

All formulas begin with an equal sign (=), and all field names are in parentheses. The following are some examples:

- To calculate a total price where a control called Quantity contains the number of items and a control called Price holds the price of each item, you would multiply these data in these two controls. The formula would look like this: **=[Quantity]\*[Price]**.

- To calculate a 25% discount off the value in the field, such as a field called Cost, you would type the formula **=[Cost]\*.075**.

- To add the total of the values in three fields, enter **[Field1]+ [Field2]+[Field3]** (where Field# is the name of the field).

**PLAIN ENGLISH**

**More Room**    If you run out of room in the text box when typing your formula, press **Shift+F2** to open a Zoom box, which gives you more room.

In this lesson, you learned how to customize your report by adding and removing controls, moving them around, and creating calculations. In the next lesson, you learn how to take advantage of table relationships in forms, queries, and reports.

# LESSON 21
# Taking Advantage of Database Relationships

*In this lesson, you learn how to view related table data and use related tables in forms and reports.*

## REVIEWING TABLE RELATIONSHIPS

When we first discussed creating a database earlier in this book, we made a case for creating tables that held discrete subsets of the data that would make up the database. We then discussed the importance of creating relationships between these tables, as discussed in Lesson 11, "Creating Relationships Between Tables." In this lesson, you take a look at how you can take advantage of related tables when creating other Access objects, such as forms, queries, and reports.

As previously discussed in Lessons 2 and 11, tables are related by a field that is common to each table. The common field serves as the primary key in one of the tables and as the foreign key in the other table. (The foreign key is the same field, but it is held in a table where it does not serve as the primary key.)

For example, in Figure 21.1, an Employees table is linked to two other tables: Expenses and Departments. The Employees table and the Expenses table are related because of the EmployeeID field. The Employees table and the Departments table are related by the DepartmentID field.

The more complex your database, the more tables and table relationships the database contains. For example, Figure 21.2 shows a complex company database that contains several related tables.

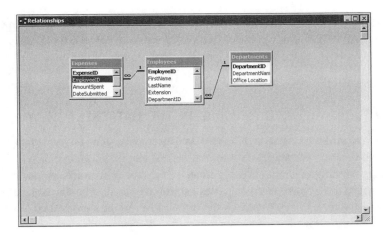

**FIGURE 21.1**
*Related tables share a common field.*

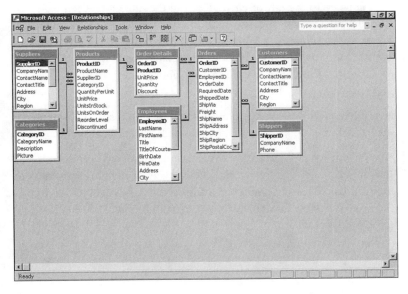

**FIGURE 21.2**
*Complex databases contain many related tables.*

More important to the discussion in this lesson is how you take advantage of related tables to create complex forms and reports. First, take a look at how related table data can be viewed in the Table Datasheet view.

## VIEWING RELATED RECORDS IN THE DATASHEET VIEW

When working with a table in the Datasheet view, you can view data held in a related table. The information that can be viewed is contained in any table that is subordinate to the table you currently have open in the Datasheet view. Tables subordinate to a particular table hold the foreign key (which is the primary key in the top-level table in the relationship).

For example, suppose you are viewing the Departments table that was included in the table relationships shown in Figure 21.1. A plus sign appears to the left of each record in the table (see Figure 21.3). To view related data for each record, click the plus sign. A table appears that contains the related data for that record. In this example, the Employees table provides the related data (which, if you look back at Figure 21.1, was related subordinately to the Departments table).

When related records are displayed, the plus sign turns into a minus sign. Click that minus sign to hide the related records again.

As you can see in Figure 21.3, even the related records can have linked information. For example, clicking any of the plus signs next to the records containing employee information shows data pulled from the Expenses table (which, again referring to Figure 21.1, is related to the Employees table).

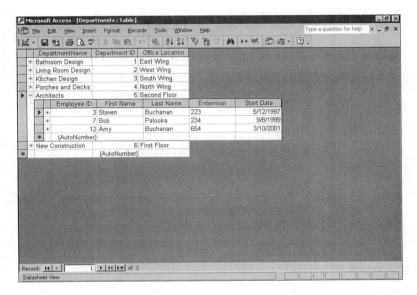

**FIGURE 21.3**
*Display related records in the linked table by clicking a plus sign next to a record.*

# CREATING MULTI-TABLE QUERIES

The real power of relational databases is to use the related tables to create other Access objects, such as queries. Multi-table queries enable you to pull information from several related tables. You can then use this query to create a report or a form.

The easiest way to create a multi-table query is in the Query Design view. Follow these steps:

1. From the database window (with the Query icon selected), double-click **Create Query in Design View**. The Show Table dialog box appears.

2. In the Show Table dialog box (see Figure 21.4), select the related tables that you want to include in the query. For example, using the tables shown in Figure 21.4, you could create a query using the Employees, Departments, and Expenses tables that would show you each employee, the department, and any expenses that the employee has incurred.

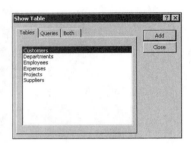

**FIGURE 21.4**
*Select the tables that will be used to create the multi-table query.*

3. After you have selected the tables for the query, click **Close** to close the Show Table dialog box. The tables and their relationships appear at the top of the Query Design window.

4. Add the fields to the Query grid that make up the query. The fields can come from any of the tables that you have included in the query. Figure 21.5 shows a multi-table query that includes fields from the Employees, Departments, and Expenses tables.

5. When you have finished designing the multi-table query, you can run it. Click the **Run** button on the toolbar.

The query results appear in the Datasheet view. Combining data from related tables into one query allows you to create other objects from that query, such as forms or reports.

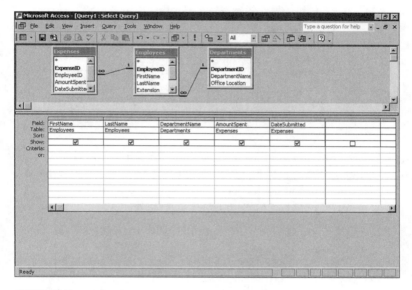

**FIGURE 21.5**
*Multi-table queries enable you to pull data from fields on more than one table.*

## CREATING MULTI-TABLE FORMS

Forms can be created from more than one table using the Form Wizard or the Form Design view. Creating a form from fields that reside in more than one table allows you to enter data into more than one table using just the single form.

A very simple way to create a multi-table form is to add a *subform* to an existing form. For example, you might have a form that is based on a Customers table. If you would also like to be able to view and enter order information when you work with the Customers form, you can add an Orders subform to it. It is important that the tables used to create the two forms (the main form and the subform) are related tables.

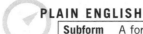

### PLAIN ENGLISH

> **Subform**    A form control that actually consists of an entire form based on another table or tables.

The easiest way to create a subform is to actually drag an existing form onto another form in the Design view. The following steps describe how you do it:

1. Use the AutoForm feature, the Form Wizard, or the Form Design view to create two forms: the form that serves as the main form and the form that serves as the subform. These forms should be based on tables that are related.

2. In the Form Design view, open the form that will serve as the main form.

3. Size the Form Design window so that you can also see the database window in the Access workspace (see Figure 21.6).

4. In the database window, be sure that the Forms list is showing. Then, drag the form that will serve as the subform onto the main form that is open in the Design view. When the mouse pointer enters the Design view, it becomes a control pointer. Release the mouse button when you are in the general area where you want to place the subform. The subform control appears on the main form.

5. Maximize the Form Design window. Reposition or size the subform in the Design view until you are happy with its location (see Figure 21.7).

6. Save the changes that you have made to the main form (specifically, the addition of the subform).

7. To change to the Form view to view or add data to the composite form, click the **View** button on the Form Design toolbar.

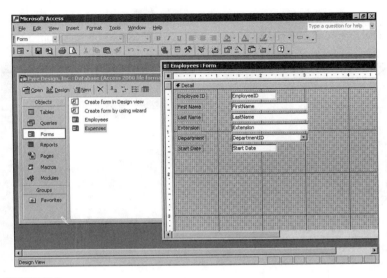

**FIGURE 21.6**
*The subform is dragged from the database window onto the Design view of the main form.*

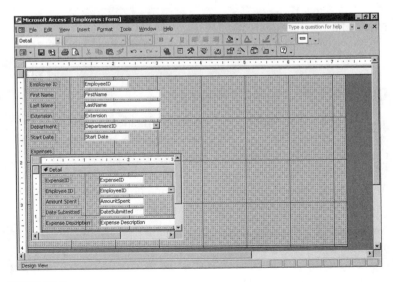

**FIGURE 21.7**
*The subform becomes another control on the main form.*

Figure 21.8 shows the main form and the subform in the Form view. The form can be used to view or enter data into two tables at once.

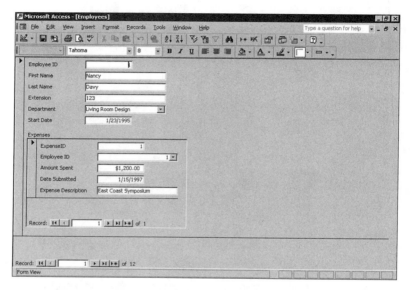

**FIGURE 21.8**
*The composite form can be used to view and enter data into more than one table.*

## CREATING MULTI-TABLE REPORTS

You can also create reports that include information from more than one table or query. The process is the same as the procedure that you used in Lesson 19, "Creating a Simple Report," when you used the Report Wizard to create a report. All you have to do is select fields from related tables during the report creation process. This allows the report to pull information from the related tables.

An alternative to creating reports that contain fields from more than one table is to create a report that contains a *subreport*. The procedure is similar to the procedure discussed in the previous section, when you created a main form that held a subform.

**PLAIN ENGLISH**

**Subreport**   A report control that consists of an entire report based on another table or tables.

To create a report that contains a subreport, follow these steps:

1.  Use the AutoReport feature, the Report Wizard, or the Report Design view to create two reports: the report that serves as the main report and the report that serves as the subreport. These reports should be based on tables that are related.

2.  In the Report Design view, open the report that will serve as the main report. Size the area in which you will place the subreport. For example, you might want to place the subreport in the Report Header area so that it can be viewed on any page of the printed report.

3.  Size the Report Design window so that you can also see the database window in the Access workspace.

4.  In the database window, be sure that the Reports list is showing. Then, drag the report that will serve as the subreport onto the main report in the Design view window. Don't release the mouse until you have positioned the mouse pointer in the area (such as the Report Header) where you want to place the subreport.

5.  Size or move the subreport control as needed and then save any changes that you have made to the main report.

When you view the composite report in the Print Preview mode, the subreport appears as part of the main report. Figure 21.9 shows the composite report in the Print Preview mode. Placing subreports on a main report enables you to include summary data that can be referenced while data on the main report is viewed either on the screen or on the printed page.

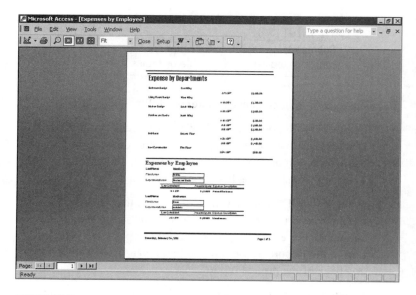

**FIGURE 21.9**
*Composite reports enable you to report the data in different ways on the same report.*

In this lesson, you learned how to create queries, forms, and reports based on more than one related table. In the next lesson, you learn how to print Access objects.

# LESSON 22
# Printing Access Objects

*In this lesson, you learn how to print Access tables, forms, queries, and reports.*

## ACCESS OBJECTS AND THE PRINTED PAGE

You have probably gotten a feel for the fact that tables, forms, and queries are used mainly to view and manipulate database information on your computer's screen, whereas the report is designed to be printed. This doesn't mean that you can't print a table or a form; it's just that the report provides the greatest amount of control in placing information on the printed page.

First, this lesson discusses printing Access objects with the report. Then, you look at printing some of the other Access objects, such as a table or form.

## PRINTING REPORTS

As you learned earlier in this book, the Access report is the ideal format for presenting database information on the printed page. Using reports, you can add page numbering controls and other header or footer information that repeat on each page of the report.

Whether you create a report using AutoReport or the Report Wizard, the completed report appears in the Print Preview mode, as shown in Figure 22.1.

 You can immediately send the report to the default printer by clicking the **Print** button on the Print Preview toolbar. If you find that you would like to change the margins on the report or change how the

report is oriented on the page, click the **Setup** button on the Print
Preview toolbar. The Page Setup dialog box appears (see Figure 22.2).

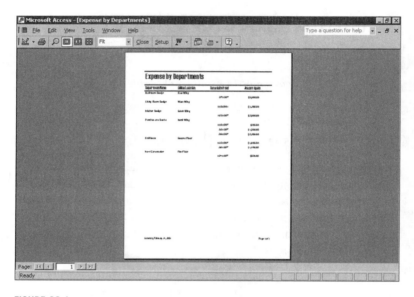

**FIGURE 22.1**
*Reports created using AutoReport or the Report Wizard open in the Print Preview mode.*

**FIGURE 22.2**
*The Page Setup dialog box enables you to control the margins and page orientation of the printed report.*

Three tabs are on the Page Setup dialog box:

- **Margins**—This tab enables you to set the top, bottom, left, and right margins. To change one of the default settings (1 inch), type the new setting in the appropriate margin box.

- **Page**—This tab enables you to change the orientation of the report on the printed page. Portrait, which is the default setting, orients the report text from top to bottom on a regular 8 1/2-inch by 11-inch page. Landscape turns the page 180 degrees, making it an 11-inch by 8 1/2-inch page. Landscape orientation works well for reports that contain a large number of fields placed from left to right on the report. This tab also enables you to select the type of paper that you are going to use for the printout (such as letter, legal, and so on).

- **Columns**—This tab enables you to change the number of columns in the report and the distance between the columns. Because the columns for the report are determined when you create the report using AutoReport or the Report Wizard, you probably won't want to tamper with the column settings. It's easier to change the distance between field controls in the Report Design view.

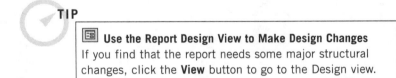

TIP

🖳 **Use the Report Design View to Make Design Changes**
If you find that the report needs some major structural changes, click the **View** button to go to the Design view.

After you have finished making your choices in the Page Setup dialog box, click **OK** to close the dialog box. You can now print the report.

## PRINTING OTHER DATABASE OBJECTS

The fastest way to print a database object, such as a table, form, or query, is to select the object in the database window. Just select the appropriate object icon in the database window and select an object in the object list, such as a table.

 After the object is selected, click the **Print** button on the database toolbar. Your database object is sent to the printer.

If you would like to preview the printout of a table, form, or query, either select the particular object in the database window or open the particular object and then click the **Print Preview** button. The object is then displayed in the Print Preview mode, such as the table shown in Figure 22.3.

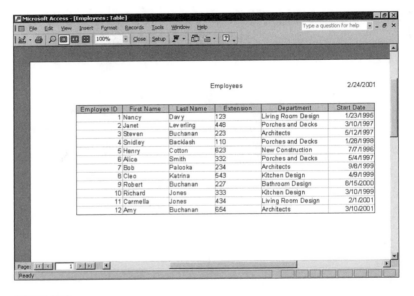

**FIGURE 22.3**
*Any database object, such as a table, can be viewed in Print Preview.*

When you print tables, forms, or queries, the name of the object and the current date are placed at the top of the printout. Page numbering is automatically placed at the bottom of the printout. You can control the margins and the page layout (portrait or landscape) for the table printout (or other object) using the Page Setup dialog box (discussed earlier in this lesson).

## USING THE PRINT DIALOG BOX

So far, this discussion of printing in Access has assumed that you want to print to your default printer. You can also print a report or other database object to a different printer and control the range of pages that are printed or the actual records that are printed. These settings are controlled in the Print dialog box.

From the Print Preview mode or with a particular object open in the Access window, select **File**, **Print**. The Print dialog box appears (see Figure 22.4).

**FIGURE 22.4**
*The Print dialog box enables you to select a different printer or specify a print range.*

To select a different printer (one other than the default), click the **Name** drop-down list and select a printer by name. If you want to select a range of pages to print (such as a range of pages in a report), click the **Pages** option button and then type the page range into the page boxes.

In the case of tables and queries, you can also print selected records. Before you open the Print dialog box, select the records in the table or query. Then, when you open the Print dialog box, click the **Selected Record(s)** option button.

When you have finished changing the default printer or specifying a page range or the printing of select records, you are ready to print the object. Click the **OK** button. This closes the Print dialog box and sends the object to the printer.

In this lesson you learned how to print the various Access objects.

# INDEX

# T

## W-X

## Y-Z